ISBN 978-0-9850031-4-2

ISSN 2157-586X

THE JOURNAL OF THE BLACK CATHOLIC THEOLOGICAL SYMPOSIUM (BCTS) was founded in 2007.

MANUSCRIPTS should be submitted to the editorial board by the deadline announced at the Annual Meeting, which is also posted at http://www.bcts.org. All submissions must be formatted in Chicago Turabian style with Works Cited page and sent via electronic mail to senior editor Kimberly Flint-Hamilton: kflintha@stetson.edu, and also to editor Cecilia Moore: Cecilia.Moore@notes.udayton.edu. For examples of Chicago Turabian style, see: http://www.press.uchicago.edu/books/turabian/turabian_citationguide.html.

The Journal of the Black Catholic Theological Symposium is composed of original articles by its members and guest contributors, and will not publish manuscripts that have been previously published elsewhere.

REVIEWS of books or films that have relevance to the Black Catholic Theological Symposium may also be submitted and will be considered for publication. Reviews originally published elsewhere will not be considered for publication.

MEMBERSHIP in the Black Catholic Theological Symposium is by invitation only. Those interested in joining the organization may review membership guidelines from Article II of the Constitution, posted on the BCTS web site: http://www.bcts.org, and contact the secretary of the BCTS, Shawnee Daniels-Sykes, SSND, at the following electronic mail address: sykess@mtmary.edu.

The opinions expressed in the articles and reviews published in *The Journal of the Black Catholic Theological Symposium* are those of the authors and are not necessarily the opinions of the editorial board, the organization, or the publisher.

The Journal of the Black Catholic Theological Symposium is provided to all paid members of the BCTS. Additional copies of the journal may be obtained by contacting the publisher, Steven Hamilton, of Fortuity Press, at the following electronic mail address: steven.hamilton@fortuitypress.com.

Fortuity Press
Copyright © 2014 by Fortuity Press LLC
All rights reserved.

This periodical is indexed in the ATLA Catholic Periodical and Literature Index® (CPLI®), a product of the American Theological Library Association, 300 S. Wacker Dr., Suite 2100, Chicago, IL 60606, USA. Email: atla@atla.com, www: http://www.atla.com.

No part of this volume may be reprinted or reproduced or utilized in any form by any electronic, mechanical, or other means, now known or hereafter invented, including photocopying and recording, or any information storage or retrieval system, without permission in writing from the publishers, except under title 17, U. S. Code, Section 107 "fair use doctrine" for academic research.

Printed in the United States of America.
Cover design by Steven Hamilton, Kimberly Flint-Hamilton
Cover photograph entitled *Sunset's Grace* by Steven Hamilton © 2014
Cover art by Steven Hamilton.
Interior design by Steven Hamilton, Kimberly Flint-Hamilton

THE JOURNAL

OF THE

BLACK CATHOLIC THEOLOGICAL SYMPOSIUM (BCTS) VOLUME EIGHT

EDITORS

Cyprian Davis, O.S.B., Editor-in-Chief
Saint Meinrad Archabbey

Kimberly Flint-Hamilton, Senior Editor
Stetson University

Cecilia Moore, Editor
University of Dayton

Diana Hayes, Book Review Editor
Georgetown University

THE BLACK CATHOLIC THEOLOGICAL SYMPOSIUM (BCTS)

2014 OFFICERS

C. Vanessa White, Convener

Kathleen Dorsey Bellow, Associate Convener

Shawnee Daniels-Sykes, SSND, Secretary

Timone Davis, Treasurer

Cyprian Davis, OSB., Archivist

Bryan Massingale, Past Convener

THE JOURNAL OF THE BCTS

Volume Eight   2014

LETTER FROM THE EDITOR

Kimberly Flint-Hamilton, Ph.D.   1
From The Editor's Desk: A Year of Many Emotions

IN MEMORIAM

Cecilia Moore, Ph.D.   13
Memorial for Father Paul M. Marshall, S.M.
(August 17, 1947 – July 17, 2014)

Fr. Joseph Brown, S.J.   17
"To See What the End Will Be"

ARTICLES

Kathleen Dorsey Bellow, D.Min.   21
The Black Community and the Call for Vatican Council II
(1962-1965)

Sr. M. Reginald Anibueze, DDL   53
Immigrants and Cultural Continuance in the Liturgy:
Celebrating the Nigerian Igbo Mass in the United
States

Nathaniel Samuel, Ph.D.   77
Building a Story Together: The Challenge of Conversion
in a Plural Age: A Narrative Interpretation

BOOK REVIEWS

Maureen R. O'Brien and Susan Yanos, editors.   95
Emerging from the Vineyard.
Essays by Lay Ecclesial Ministers.
(C. V. White)

Anthony B. Pinn   99
Introducing African American Religion.
(L. Mosely)

Yolanda Flores, Angela Harris,   103
Gabriela Gutierrez y Muhs and Carmen Gonzales, editors.
Presumed Incompetent: The Intersections of Race
and Class for Women in Academia.
(R. Lee)

CHRONOLOGY
BCTS Annual Meetings   107

FROM THE EDITOR'S DESK: A YEAR OF MANY EMOTIONS

Kimberly Flint-Hamilton, Ph.D.
Stetson University
DeLand, Florida

So much has happened in the year 2014. For many, we experienced this year as a roller coaster of thoughts and emotions.

2014 marks a year of remembrance as we celebrate another important anniversary. Fifty years ago, in 1964, Pope Paul VI promulgated the Vatican II document *Lumen Gentium* (Light of Nations), The Dogmatic Constitution of the Church.

We were elated when we celebrated the first dual canonization of pontiffs in Church history. On Sunday April 27th, Pope Francis canonized John XXIII, who called for the Second Vatican Council, and John Paul II.[1]

Two months later, on June 21st, Pope Francis surprised us, using "his strongest language to date" to excommunicate members of the Italian mafia.[2]

We rejoiced in celebration as, after a national search, the Institute for Black Catholic Studies at Xavier University in New Orleans named Fr. Maurice Nutt, CSs R as its new director. The IBCS is thrice-blessed to have Fr. Nutt in this role. Not only is Fr. Nutt an active member of the BCTS; he's also both an alumnus and faculty member of the IBCS. Fr. Nutt joins a long history of extraordinary IBCS leaders, including Fr. Dr. Thaddeus Posey, OFM Cap, Fr. Joseph Nearon, SSS, Fr. Dr. Joseph

---

[1] Laura Smith-Spark, Delia Gallagher and Ben Wedeman, "Sainthood for John Paul II and John XXIII as Crowds Pack St. Peter's Square." *CNN World*, April 28th, 2014, accessed September 14, 2014, http://www.cnn.com/2014/04/27/world/pope-canonization/.

[2] Delia Gallagher, "Pope Excommunicates Italian Mobsters." *CNN Belief Blog*, June 21, 2014, accessed September 12, 2014, http://religion.blogs.cnn.com/2014/06/21/pope-excommunicates-mafia-members/. See also Alexander Stille, "The Pope Excommunicates the Mafia, Finally," *The New Yorker*, June 21, 2014, accessed September 21, 2014, http://www.newyorker.com/news/daily-comment/the-pope-excommunicates-the-mafia-finally.

Brown, SJ, Sr. Dr. Eva Regina Martin, SSF, and Sr. Dr. Jamie Phelps, OP. True to form, Fr. Nutt thought long and prayed deeply, before agreeing to follow in the footsteps of these notable leaders. "He didn't take lightly the invitation to be director, discerning for six weeks 'because I wanted to know if this was where God was calling me,' he said. 'I felt God was trying to use me.'" [3] The BCTS celebrates Fr. Nutt in his new position and looks forward to many years of growth and success.

Fr. Maurice Nutt, CSsR[4]

Yet, despite our joy following Fr. Nutt's first successful summer, anger and frustration gripped us as, on August 9th,

---

[3] "Fr. Nutt to Lead Institute for Black Catholic Studies," *The St. Louis American*, May 1, 2014, accessed September 21, 2014, http://www.stlamerican.com/religion/local_religion/article_13376090-d0a5-11e3-b493-0019bb2963f4.html. See also Christine Bordelon, "Institute of Black Catholic Studies Has New Director," *The Clarion Herald*, July 15, 2014, accessed September 7, 2014, http://clarionherald.info/clarion/index.php/special-sections/back-to-school/3524-institute-of-black-catholic-studies-had-new-director#sthash.vN8Te7I6.dpuf; and "History," *The Institute for Black Catholic Studies*, accessed September 21, 2014, http://www.xula.edu/ibcs/documents/History.pdf.

[4] Photo provided by Maurice Nutt.

2014, unarmed teen Michael Brown was shot six times and killed by police at 12:01 pm in Ferguson, Missouri. Rioting in Ferguson ensued for weeks thereafter. Since 9/11, an estimated 5000 civilians have been killed by police in the U.S., and most of the victims have been black or Hispanic, killed by white police.[5] U.S. police shoot and kill an average of 409 people per year. Compare this with statistics from the U.K. Between 2010 and 2014, police officers in England and Wales shot and killed a total of 7 people.[6] According to one social activist organization, the Malcolm X Grassroots Movement, "police officers, security guards or self-appointed vigilantes killed at least 313 Black people in 2012 — meaning one Black person was killed in the U.S. by law enforcement roughly every 28 hours."[7] We still have far to go in the quest for racial justice.

Anxiety filled our hearts and minds with the news about the African Ebola epidemic. Several West African nations are experiencing the greatest outbreak of Ebola since it was first documented in 1976, with more than 1400 deaths and 2600 infected.[8] With only four pharmaceutical companies producing vaccines today compared to 26 companies five decades ago, we may be a year or more away from an effective, clinically-tested cure.[9]

---

[5] Katie Rucke, "US Police Have Killed More Than 5000 Civilians Since 2011" *MintPress News,* November 6, 2013, accessed September 21, 2014, http://www.mintpressnews.com/us-police-murdered-5000-innocent-civilians-since-911/172029/.

[6] D.K., "Armed Police, Trigger Happy," *The Economist,* August 14, 2014, accessed September 17, 2014, http://www.economist.com/blogs/democracyinamerica/2014/08/armed-police.

[7] Rucke, *op. cit.* See also "Report, Operation Ghetto Storm 2012," *Malcolm X Grassroots Movement,* accessed September 21, 2014, http://mxgm.org/category/media/newsletter/operation-ghetto-storm-2012-annual-report-on-the-extrajudicial-killing-of-313-black-people/.

[8] "Ebola Outbreak: US Official Says Epidemic Will Worsen," *BBC News Africa,* August 27, 2014, accessed September 14, 2014, http://www.bbc.com/news/world-africa-28961944?print=true.

[9] Donna Dickenson, "The Ethics of Ebola," *News Vision, Uganda's Leading Daily,* September 7, 2014, accessed September 14, 2014, http://www.newvision.co.ug/news/659577-the-ethics-of-ebola.html.

A wave of excitement washed over the Oral History Team as Cecilia Moore, Steve Hamilton and I drove from Astor Florida, to Athens Georgia, to Memphis Tennessee, to Belleville Illinois, to Chicago Illinois, and back again to interview four notable "firsts" in the Oral History Project. Diane Batts Morrow was the first married interviewee; Fr. James Herring O. Praem. was the first interviewee who took his vows after a lengthy secular career – he was in his 50s when he became a priest – Bishop Terry Steib SVD and Bishop Edward Braxton were the first bishops.

And we felt a sense of sadness and loss as we bade farewell to two members of the BCTS family, former IBCS director Sr. Dr. Eva Regina Martin SSF and Fr. Paul Marshall SM. Ironically, the Oral History Team had been discussing tentative plans earlier this year to interview both.

Sr. Eva Regina left a deep impression on her religious community, fellow BCTS members and the IBCS community, as attested in the following comments:[10]

---

[10] Quotes from Xavier University Institute for Black Catholic Studies Guestbook, Sister Eva Regina Martin S.S.F., accessed September 21, 2014, http://www.xula.edu/ibcs/documents/TributetoSrEvaReginaMartinSSF.pdf.

Sr. Eva Regina Martin, SSF[11]

On your pilgrim journey in such amazing ways your spirit exuded so much love, light, and leadership. You touched thousands of people in our Church, society, and world. In profound and creative ways you captured and illuminated the multidimensional experiences of Black Catholics, those alive and those who have passed onto glory. I will never go to the French Quarters and walk past the black wrought iron fences, railings, and gates again without remembering you and your academic and scholarly contributions about that history. I am honored and privileged to have known you over the many years. I am so inspired by your powerful legacy!

Dr. Shawnee Daniels-Sykes, SSND
Associate Professor of Theology
Mount Mary University

Sr. Eva Regina Martin, SSF was indeed a woman of great faith and dedication to all whom she serve. Her leadership as Director of the Institute (1997-2003) was creative and steadfast. Her special

---

[11] Photo courtesy of the Clarion Herald.

affection for the elderly was palpable as her own Holy Family sisters will attest. Because of who she was and how she lived her life, I have no doubt that she is already doing *the second line in heaven*. She joins the dance of praise with the other Holy Family Sisters who entered eternal life, before her and our other venerable ancestors of the Institute especially our saintly icon Sr. Thea Bowman, the other deceased directors and faculty (Joseph Nearon SSS, Thaddeus Posey OFM Cap, Clarence Rivers, "Mothers of the Institute": Elencie Shynes [Momma Shynes], Mabel Turner [Mamma Mabel], Vivian Roussan [Momma Roussan], and students (Duane Brown, Alice Spurlock, and Corita Loving) and other deceased faculty, staff, and students of the Institute.

Dr. Jamie T. Phelps, OP
Former IBCS Director (2003-2011)

When I found out that Sr. Eva Regina had passed away, my thoughts immediately went back to the last time I saw her in my office. She came by to drop off a book that we had asked to borrow. As always, she walked into the office with a big smile, gave me the book and said, "I want my book back when y'all are done, this is the only one I have and it's like my second bible." She was just so comical, but very thoughtful and always willing to help out anywhere she can, especially with the Institute for Black Catholic Studies. The IBCS was one of her passions and she would always make herself available to help out in any way she could. She made sure that she would send two or three of the Holy Family Sisters to our summer program each year. I will miss her very dearly. Rest in Peace Sister Eva Regina Martin, SSF.

Loretta D. Salomon
Institute for Black Catholic Studies
Xavier University of Louisiana

We, The National Black Catholic Congress, wish to express our sincere sympathy on the death of Sr. Eva Regina Martin, SSF. We give thanks to Almighty God for have given us such a gift; a woman of service, a woman of faith, a woman of God. We loved her, but God loved her even more. There is cause for rejoicing here because Sr. Eva Regina blessed our lives in so many ways.

Valerie Washington
Executive Director
National Black Catholic Congress

Sr. Dr. Jamie T. Phelps, OP with Sr. Eva Regina[12]

---

[12] Photo by Kathleen Dorsey Bellow, D.Min.

Fr. Paul Marshall too is remembered fondly by his colleagues in the BCTS and by community:

Fr. Paul Marshall, SM[13]

Know that I will remember Paul, his colleagues and religious congregation in my thoughts and prayers. I recall him being in one of my theology classes at Catholic Theological Union during one of his sabbaticals. I was impressed with his theological foundation and critical insights – he was a seminarian who took his M.Div. studies seriously! In short, he was a loving person and priest, who seriously sought ongoing theological knowledge as a foundation for his ministry and spiritual journey.

Sr. Dr. Jamie T. Phelps OP
Former IBCS Director (2003-2011)

---

[13] Photo courtesy of University of Dayton.

I knew and loved Fr. Paul for many years as friend, priest, teacher, colleague, and advocate. We grew together from pre-NBCC 1987, to years of support to Operation Good News, to his uplifting words this year during my mother's final days. Always, he was a clear sign of Christ's love-in-action!!! RIP dear friend, your BEST friend, Jesus is nigh.

Claudine Pannell-Goodlett
BCTS Member

Let us thank God for the gift of his life and the many ways he blessed our University community. Let us thank Mary Our Mother for the gift of his perseverance as a Marianist religious. Together, let us pray that he may rest in the peace of Christ.

Fr. James Fitz, SM[14]
University of Dayton
Vice President for Mission and Rector

Paul's death is a great loss to the Province and for the Marianist Family. Please pray for him now and thank God for this wonderful religious and brother.

Fr. Martin Solma, SM[15]
Marianist Provincial

This year's Journal features three exciting papers and three book reviews. Kathleen Dorsey Bellow's article, "The Black Community and the Call for Vatican Council II (1962-1965)," comes at the 50th anniversary of the promulgation of *Lumen Gentium*. Nathaniel Samuel's paper, "Building a Story Together – The Challenge of Conversion in a Plural Age," explores the concept of the practice of narrative hospitality. Sr. Reginald Anibueze, DDL's paper, "Immigrants and Cultural Continuance in the Liturgy: Celebrating the Nigerian Igbo Mass in the United

---

[14] "In Memoriam: Fr. Paul Marshall," *University of Dayton News*, July 17, 2014, accessed September 22, 2014, https://www.udayton.edu/news/articles/2014/07/in_memoriam_former_rector_paul_marshall.php.

[15] "Death of Fr. Paul Marshall, S.M.," *The Marianists*, July 17, 2014, accessed September 22, 2014, http://www.marianist.com/?p=18908.

States," describes the liturgical life of the Nigerian Catholic community in the United States. We also include three book reviews: LaReine-Marie Mosely's review of Anthony Pinn's *Introducing African American Religion* (Routledge, 2013), Roy Lee's review of Yonalda Flores, et al., *Presumed Incompetent: The Intersections of Race and Class for Women in Academia* (Utah State University Press, 2012), and Vanessa White's review of O'Brien and Yanos' *Emerging from the Vineyard. Essays by Lay Ecclesial Ministers* (Fortuity Press, 2014). Also included is a touching poem in memory of Sr. Eva Regina Martin by Fr. Joseph Brown SJ entitled "To See What the End Will Be," and a memorial essay for Fr. Paul Marshall by Cecilia Moore.

Works Cited

BBC News Africa. "Ebola Outbreak: US Official Says Epidemic Will Worsen." August 27, 2014. Accessed September 14, 2014 http://www.bbc.com/news/world-africa-28961944?print=true.

Bordelon, Christine. "Institute of Black Catholic Studies Has New Director." *The Clarion Herald*, July 15, 2014. Accessed September 7, 2014. http://clarionherald.info/clarion/index.php/special-sections/back-to-school/3524-institute-of-black-catholic-studies-had-new-director#sthash.vN8Te7I6.dpuf.

D.K., "Armed Police, Trigger Happy." *The Economist,* August 14, 2014. Accessed September 17, 2014. http://www.economist.com/blogs/democracyinamerica/2014/08/armed-police.

Gallagher, Delia. "Pope Excommunicates Italian Mobsters." *CNN Belief Blog*, June 21, 2014. Accessed September 12, 2014. http://religion.blogs.cnn.com/2014/06/21/pope-excommunicates-mafia-members/.

Institute for Black Catholic Studies, The. "History." Accessed September 21, 2014. http://www.xula.edu/ibcs/documents/History.pdf.

Malcolm X Grassroots Movement. "Report, Operation Ghetto Storm 2012." Accessed September 21, 2014. http://mxgm.org/category/media/newsletter/operation-ghetto-storm-2012-annual-report-on-the-extrajudicial-killing-of-313-black-people/.

Marianists, The. "Death of Fr. Paul Marshall, S.M." July 17, 2014. Accessed September 22, 2014. http://www.marianist.com/?p=18908.

St. Louis American, The. "Fr. Nutt to Lead Institute for Black Catholic Studies." May 1, 2014. Accessed September 21, 2014. http://www.stlamerican.com/religion/local_religion/article_13376090-d0a5-11e3-b493-0019bb2963f4.html.

University of Dayton News. "In Memoriam: Fr. Paul Marshall." July 17, 2014. Accessed September 22, 2014. https://www.udayton.edu/news/articles/2014/07/in_memoriam_former_rector_paul_marshall.php.

Rucke, Katie. "US Police Have Killed More Than 5000 Civilians Since 2011." *MintPress News,* November 6, 2013. Accessed September 21, 2014. http://www.mintpressnews.com/us-police-murdered-5000-innocent-civilians-since-911/172029/.

Smith-Spark, Laura, Delia Gallagher and Ben Wedeman. "Sainthood for John Paul II and John XXIII as Crowds Pack St. Peter's Square." *CNN World,* April 28th, 2014. Accessed September 14, 2014. http://www.cnn.com/2014/04/27/world/pope-canonization/.

Stille, Alexander. "The Pope Excommunicates the Mafia, Finally." *The New Yorker,* June 21, 2014. Accessed September 21, 2014. http://www.newyorker.com/news/daily-comment/the-pope-excommunicates-the-mafia-finally.

Xavier University Institute for Black Catholic Studies Guestbook. "Sister Eva Regina Martin S.S.F." Accessed September 21, 2014. http://www.xula.edu/ibcs/documents/TributetoSrEvaReginaMartinSSF.pdf.

Memorial for Father Paul M. Marshall, S.M.
(August 17, 1947 – July 17, 2014)

Cecilia Moore, Ph.D.
University of Dayton
Dayton, Ohio

Father Paul Marshall, S.M. was born at the right time – the right time for a black man in the Catholic Church to pursue his priestly vocation. As a baby boomer, he came of age during the civil rights movement and Vatican II. These two factors uniquely positioned him to pursue his passion for freedom and faith in the black community. From childhood his vocation was evident to family and friends. His sister, Iris Marshall Brown, recalls among Father Marshall's favorite things to do was to play Mass. Even though Paul was one of the youngest of the siblings (there were six children born to Isaiah and Donia Marshall), he always was the priest when they played Mass. The family's fine table linens served as his altar cloth and vestments on many occasions in the Marshall household much to the chagrin of his mother who taught home economics. While Paul may have faced some scolding for rumpling the linens, he received even more loving support and encouragement as he determined early in life that what he played at he would one day be – a priest.

Father Marshall professed his first vows as a Marianist (Society of Mary) in 1966 and was ordained to the priesthood in 1976. In his 47 years as a Marianist brother and priest, Father Marshall's ministries included social work, high school and university teaching, parish pastor (17 years at St. Aloysius Church in Cleveland, Ohio, his hometown), rector of the University of Dayton, and assistant for temporalities for the Marianist Province of the United States. It was in his role as assistant for temporalities that he travelled to Ranchi, India where he died suddenly and quietly on July 17, 2014. Father Marshall took on all these ministries with a true sense of joy and commitment.

One outstanding quality of his life was he that he was sincerely happy and at peace with the choices he made in his life, especially his choice to join the Marianists. On the occasion of his 25th jubilee as a Marianist, Paul said, "The Marianists have always been open to someone of a different culture. Our life together, I believe, is a witness to the kingdom of God. Every race, culture and people are called to be followers of God. Mary, our model of faith, praised God who raised the lowly and freed the oppressed. Working for freedom and promoting the faith in the black community have given meaning to my life as a Marianist."[1]

Father Marshall found happiness and purpose in being a black Catholic. He was both a member and a president of the National Black Catholic Clergy Caucus and a member of the Black Catholic Theological Symposium. In his ministry as pastor he infused black spirituality, homiletics, and sacred music in the Mass. He worked closely with the late Archbishop James P. Lyke when he was in Cleveland on a host of issues that were of spiritual, economic, political, moral, and social consequence in the black community. Father Marshall[2] was a member of the faculty of the Institute for Black Catholic Studies. He, Cecilia Moore, and Emily Strand instituted the  Annual Father Joseph M. Davis, S.M. Black Catholic History Month Celebration at the University of Dayton in 2005. Father Marshall was an activist for food security for people around the globe in his work as a member of the national board of Bread for the World. His scholarship on spirituality served the black

---

[1] "Former UD Rector, Father Paul Marshall, Has Died," *Dayton Daily News*, 17 July 2014. http://www.daytondailynews.com/news/news/local/former-ud-rector-father-paul-marshall... (Accessed 13 September 2014.)

[2] Celebrating Mass. Photo courtesy of University of Dayton.

Catholic and wider Catholic community in his many lectures, retreats and articles on the subject. With C. Vanessa White and Cecilia Moore, Father Marshall was a co-editor of *Songs of Our Hearts and Meditations of Our Souls: Prayers for Black Catholics*. In his introduction to the prayer book, he wrote:

> Authentic prayer emerges from the interior of a person, and the transformative power of prayer takes root within the soul and grows or influences one's being. It is at this level that prayer takes on a human perspective that easily transfers to others. Authentic prayer may start with an individual's experience, and it is real. This reality invites others to contemplate their experience and connect or relate to the expression of prayer. Although prayer is born in subjectivity, it becomes the objective once expressed for others. This is the power of prayer. Prayer changes things and people.[3]

Members of the Black Catholic Theological Symposium were blessed by the many, many gifts that Paul Marshall gave over the years from his gracious hosting of the annual meeting in 2001 (and all the delicious lunches he prepared), to the insightful comments and suggestions he offered to fellow scholars at symposium gatherings on their works-in-progress, to his deep connection to the Spirit, to his bright smile and sincere embrace of welcome. Though most were not able to attend his funeral, loving messages from around the country have given comfort to his family.

We give God thanks for our brother, Father Paul Marshall, S.M. and we ask God to continue to comfort all who mourn him, especially his siblings Iris, Isaiah (Kit) and Aaron and members of the worldwide Marianist family.

---

[3] Paul M. Marshall, "Introduction to African American Spirituality," in *Songs of Hearts and Meditations of Our Souls: Prayers for Black Catholics* edited by Cecilia A. Moore, C. Vanessa White and Paul M. Marshall, S.M. (Cincinnati, OH: St. Anthony Messenger Press, 2006), xv.

Photos by Msgr. Patrick Wells

"To See What the End Will Be"

(*In honor of Sr. Eva Regina Martin, SSF, 1939-2014*)

By Fr. Joseph Brown, S.J.

I.

No

They told the first one
                               and then
year after year another   no   until
the house was built   the clothes were
stitched   the old castaways   and the invisible
babies were fed   and soothed

and then
                there were enough faces to form
a choir of hope   healing their own hearts   they
twisted scorn into praise
                           and then
dispossessed into the wilderness
they planted   harvested   and shared among
the restless wandering spirits
a little light   a little music   and
little by little
                    the world found them
and then   they all said   yes

II.

                         it was how
she walked up the path
                         mother prayers
grandmother secrets   the dreams
of babies had been rolled up carefully
in remnants from the quilts   packed
into the satchel
                  she dragged along

III.

Teaching
        touching holding more
tightly the very ones most afraid
                            the world
became a festival of heroes   where not
even dreams could root

But when the lightning flashed that summer morning
And the corrupted sermon that had long silenced
The mother-wisdom and ways of her house
came hurtling back the air
                      she screamed
her loss
            another old woman
                            (placed there
I know   by the one who refused English to ever
touch her teeth)
                said, "But you learned it all
any way you could"

IV.

The satchel

once again
            went away
                        and came back
overflowing for our feast

Was she conjure woman?
                      Yes.
No one
        knew how deep her eyes
could see

the   yes   that was merely static
in the streets
               spoke loudly in
iron stone remnants beads and feathers
and whispers never failed to satisfy

and now it is our   no   that we know

fallen to the floor
                        we demanded the miracle
that exhausted her
                        at the last

And no was prayed and sung and caressed
In the vigil of those weeping before the tomb
was readied

Until

the first one
flung the light
and dissolved the shadowed room
                                    reaching

her hand   she said   *now*
and the gentle sister of us all

said

       yes

              yes

—Luke
9 April 2014

Clarion Herald photo by Frank J. Methe

Sr. Mary Eva Regina Martin, SSF. *Born in Grand Coteau, Louisiana, in 1939. Entered the Congregation of the Sisters of the Holy Family on September 8, 1959, professed First Vows on August 15, 1962, and Perpetual Vows August 15, 1967. Masters in Black Theology from Xavier University. Doctorate in African American Studies from Temple University (1994). Educator and Administrator of Catholic schools in Louisiana and Texas. Curator, Archivist, Consultant. Sr. Eva Regina was elected to leadership in her Community and served as a General Councilor, Vicar General, and succumbed to death, April 7, 2014, while presiding in office as Congregational Leader.*

Sr. Eva Regina with Dr. C. Vanessa White[1]

---

[1] Photo by Kathleen Dorsey Bellow, D.Min.

The Black Community and the Call for Vatican Council II (1962-1965)

Kathleen Dorsey Bellow, D.Min.
Lake Charles, Louisiana

Abstract: Even as the Church celebrates the 50th anniversary of Vatican Council II (1962-65), the people of God have not unfolded much of its meaning for Catholic pastoral practice and teaching. In the excitement of Council developments, many updates were implemented in the life of the church without proper catechesis, leaving many of the faithful – proponents and opponents of the Council - wholly uninformed about the continuity of Council reforms with Catholic tradition. The dialogue between the Church and contemporary society formally endorsed in Vatican II is ongoing. A review of the world's situation in the 1950s and 60s provides perspective on the social unrest and cultural change that inspired Pope John XIII, with prompting from the Holy Ghost, to convene an ecumenical council. This essay will ground the Second Vatican Council in the context of the mid-twentieth century, with a particular focus on Black America and Black Catholic liturgical reform, to grasp a sense of its ongoing relevance for the faithful of today.

Keywords: Black Community, Vatican Council II, Black Catholic Liturgical Reform, Pope John XXIII, Zairean Rite and Clarence Rivers

> The period running roughly from 1954 to 1968 is marked indelibly with the blood, prayer, and tears of men and women of all races and all faiths who gave themselves, once again, to the struggle to win basic civil rights for the black men and women of our nation. This was the period of the 1954 Supreme Court decision on school integration, of the Montgomery bus boycott of 1955, the Freedom Rides, sit-ins, and non-violent protest. This was the time of Cicero, Watts, Detroit, and Memphis. Indeed, this was a period that so decisively shifted the relations between blacks and whites in the

United States that it may be described aptly as axial.[1]

Global Signs of the Times: Social Revolution

At all times, the Church carries the responsibility of reading the signs of the time and of interpreting them in the light of the gospel, if it is to carry out its task. In language intelligible to every generation, she should be able to answer the ever recurring questions which men ask about the meaning of this present life and the life to come, and how one is related to the other. We must be aware of and understand the aspirations, the yearnings, and the often dramatic features of the world in which we live.[2]

The signs of the times in the mid-20th century pointed to an astounding cultural revolution that threatened to turn the world community on its axis. Science and technology contributed in major ways to radical social change that, even as they conceivably improved the quality of human existence, challenged long-held conventions and values, raised new and different questions about life, faith and identity. In the give and take of societal change, it was inevitable that relationships between blacks and whites would also shift.

By the 1950s, television had become the main source of news and entertainment for many households. Through powerful marketing, McDonald's, Elvis and Playboy had made their way into the national vocabulary and helped change family consumption patterns. New medications, including the polio vaccine, oral contraception and antibiotics, were discovered.

Space travel was a breathtakingly modern field that demanded ever-new engineering, mechanical and electronic innovations. Computerization resulted in previously unheard of

---

[1] M. Shawn Copeland, "A Cadre of Women Religious Committed to Black Liberation: The National Black Sisters' Conference", *U.S. Catholic Historian* 14 (1996): 125.

[2] *Gaudium et Spes, Vatican Council II: The Conciliar and Post Conciliar Documents,* ed. Austin Flannery, O.P., (Boston: Daughters of St. Paul, 1988), #4, 905.

applications and automations. The hydrogen bomb, an "improvement" upon World War II nuclear weaponry, consolidated the deadly arsenal of the military-industrial complex. Armed forces around the world were the major patrons and beneficiaries of the astonishing technological and scientific advancements that occurred in the years 1950-70.

It is no surprise that in that era, war and the prospect of war triggered great anxiety in the world community. The Cold War gave rise to a nuclear arms race and the need for international espionage, nuclear bomb tests, home and school shelters. In addition to Cold War tensions, actual warfare raged in the Middle East, Africa and Asia. Political hostilities provoked social unrest in hotspots throughout the world.

The people of God responded variously to these complicating signs of the time.[3] They shed blood, they prayed and they cried. Their prayers and tears expressed joy and flowed in response to the sheer hardness of life. The people also stood up and spoke out. They shouted and marched in grassroots movements – large and small - that sprung up around the globe. People sat-in, demonstrated, and organized to make their various points. Opposing camps protested loudly for and against the cause of war on its many fronts. Nations in Africa, Central America and Europe fought for independence against colonial powers. There were civil rights movements for equality; the U.S. struggle described in the passage above is but one example. Women organized to oppose male-dominated systems and oppressive social structures. Young people and students joined in countless protest campaigns. Poor people world-wide pressed for economic justice. Environmentalists railed against capitalists and industrialists whose management of natural resources put the natural world at risk. Workers united to demand greater participation in the systems of commerce sustained by their labor. In the 1960 uproar of

---

[3] "Lumen Gentium", *Vatican Council II: The Conciliar and Post Conciliar Documents,* ed. Austin Flannery, O.P., (Boston: Daughters of St. Paul, 1988), #13, 364. The use of the term "God's people" refers to the following quote from the Constitution: "The one people of God is accordingly present in all the nations of the earth, since its citizens, who are taken from all nations, are of a kingdom whose nature is not earthly but heavenly."

modern social revolution, these and other popular movements took root and disorder radiated through society. To varying degrees, institutions, communities and families found everyday life turned upside down and inside out. The clash between cultural and counter-cultural ideas and values raised new questions about life with no easy answers. The people of God had become a sign of the times.

John XXII: Time for a Council

In the course of his life, Cardinal Angelo Roncalli was well-trained to read the signs of the times – the popular movements, advancements in science and technology, and the situations of war - in the light of the Gospel. Born in 1881 in northern Italy near Bergamo, the third of thirteen children in a peasant family, Roncalli envisioned the priesthood as a way to help the poor. He had no other ecclesiastical ambition. However, his natural intellect and talent were recognized and in 1901 he was sent to Rome for theological studies. The following year, he was drafted into the Italian army where he rose quickly to the rank of sergeant. When Angelo was ordained in 1904, his family could not afford the travel to Rome.[4]

After ordination, he served from 1905-14 as secretary to the bishop of Bergamo and taught in the local seminary. Drafted again during World War I as a medical orderly, Roncalli soon became a hospital chaplain. On balance, his family and life experiences were as influential in shaping his approach to ministry as the more privileged world of the seminary and bishop's office.

In 1921, Benedict XV made Angelo Roncalli national director of the Congregation for the Propagation of the Faith. By 1925, he was drafted by Pius XI into the Vatican diplomatic corps; he served in Bulgaria (1925-34), Turkey and Greece (1934-1944) with a distinguished and affectionate outreach to the Orthodox Christian churches. The diplomat Roncalli also quietly provided cover for the Jewish community during the

---

[4] John W. O'Malley, *A History of the Popes: From Peter to the Present* (Lanham: Rowman and Littlefield Publishers, Inc., 2010), 292-9; J.N.D. Kelly, *The Oxford Dictionary of Popes* (Oxford: Oxford University Press, 2005), 292.

German occupation of Greece. In these diplomatic posts, now Archbishop Roncalli spent twenty years outside Roman Catholic circles, building ecumenical alliances and working boldly across cultures.

In 1944, he was appointed papal nuncio to France. This appointment became particularly challenging after World War II due to the fact that many French clergy and prelates had taken sides during the great conflict. By most accounts, the archbishop successfully led the local church through a potentially explosive situation with considerable wisdom and negotiation skill.[5] According to Vatican II scholar, Bill Huebsch,

> In France, Roncalli also learned about the Church's needs in a "new world" whose political and spiritual lives had to be rebuilt in the wake of a devastating war. He witnessed the experimental "worker priest" movement in France, was aware of the new theology brewing in that part of Europe and involved himself personally in the question of whether the Church there in France, or indeed, in all of modern Europe would continue to decline or would experience rebirth.[6]

In 1953, he was named cardinal and patriarch of Venice, "where he was noted for his pastoral zeal, informality, and firm resistance to communist manoeuvres."[7] At long last, "at age seventy-four, he would be able to enjoy pastoral work which had been his lifelong dream. In Venice, he polished his skills at administration, equipping himself to deal eventually with the many complex administrative problems at the Vatican, especially those associated with the calling of a council."[8]

After the death of Pius XII in 1958, Cardinal Roncalli was elected pope by the College of Cardinals.[9] Shortly after his

---

[5] Ibid, 320-2; Bill Huebsch, *Vatican II in Plain English: The Council* (Allen: Thomas More Publishing, 1997), 188-90.

[6] Huebsch, 189-90.

[7] Kelly, 321.

[8] Ibid, 190.

[9] John XXIII was elected on the 12th ballot of the October 25-28 conclave. "The consensus was that he would be a transitional pope, a congenial caretaker whom both the reformers and conservatives in the

election, prompted by the Holy Spirit, John XXIII made plans to convene an Ecumenical Council.[10] The Pope persevered, despite internal resistance, in his desire that the Council affect an *aggiornamento* – an opening of the Catholic Church to the modern world, an engagement of the world with the Church, for a broader, more effective proclamation of the Good News of Salvation. He declared, "(t)he greatest concern of the ecumenical Council is that the sacred deposit of Christian doctrine should be guarded and taught more effectively...the Church should never depart from the sacred treasure of truth...But at the same time she must ever look to the present, to the new conditions and the new forms of life introduced into the modern world."[11]

This work will review historical moments in the African American community that were among contemporary signs of the times that may have stirred in Angelo Roncalli the urgent need for ecumenical dialogue that prompted the Second Vatican Council. This reflection is offered in a continuing effort to make more tangible connections between the everyday lives of African American faithful and the mission of the church universal that was stated in modern terms in the powerful gathering, interactions and documents of that Council. It is hoped that by looking back and across historical timelines in this way we might gain greater clarity of vision of who we are as God's beloved and

---

Church could accept at the time." Francis Rooney, *The Global Vatican: An Inside Look at the Catholic Church, World Politics and the Extraordinary Relationship Between the United States and the Holy See* (Lanham: Sheed & Ward, 2013), 118.

[10] The word ecumenical as used in this work connotes "universal." Huebsch, *The Council,* 53.

[11] "*Pope John XIII's Opening Address to the Second Vatican Council*" (1962). "The pope's prophetic gift was to see below the surface of the apparent triumph of midcentury Roman Catholicism: seminaries and convents around the world were overflowing with recruits; missionary priests and nuns in Africa and Latin America were moving into the postcolonial vacuum; the Cold War struggle with Communism had validated Catholic politics, with Asian figures like the Diem family in Viet Nam, leaders like Konrad Adenauer in Germany and Charles de Gaulle in France, with even Protestant America having just elected John F. Kennedy as president." James Carroll, "Introduction: The Beginning of Change" in *Vatican II: The Essential Texts (*New York: Image Books, 2012), 17.

how we are called as a community with others to be Good News in the world.

This work began with a panorama of change that transformed society at-large in the mid-twentieth century followed by a brief introduction to the man Angelo Roncalli (now St. John XXIII[12]) who was spiritually compelled to convene the Second Vatican Council. The next section will highlight historical, social, political, economic and racial events that represent "aspirations, yearnings and dramatic features" of the Black community of the 1950s and 1960s. The reflection continues with a summary of Vatican II that draws connections between the rationale and mission of the Council and the life and mission of Black Americans. The conclusion sketches two instances of Black Catholic initiative that exemplify 1) the 20th century cultural transformation that created the need for Vatican Council II and 2) local responses to the 1960s cultural divide between the people of God and the universal church that predate the Council but brilliantly connect with its teachings and outcomes.

Signs of the Time: Black Cultural, Social and Religious Change

Post-World War II was a period of economic prosperity in the United States due largely to government investment in infrastructure, including highway expansions and schools, in veteran benefits in the form of the G.I Bill that provided access to higher education and home ownership to multitudes of Americans who never before had such opportunities, and in continued military spending that supported the Cold War. A peacetime baby boom also drove up the sale of consumer goods and pushed new housing growth out into the suburbs.[13] The

---

[12] The Pope, now St. John XXIII, was canonized in April 2014.

[13] James M. O'Toole, *The Faithful: A History of Catholics in America* (Cambridge: Belknap Press of Harvard University Press, 2008), 193-8. The author also provides insight into the shift in religious and sacramental fervor that occurred in the U.S. Catholic community after World War II. The following chapter focuses on the effects of Vatican II on the U.S. Catholic faithful. See also Jay Nolan's edited work, *A History from 1850 to the Present: The American Catholic Parish, Volume 1: The Northeast, Southeast and South Central States* (Mahwah: Paulist Press, 1987).

white middle class was becoming upwardly mobile. Progress in the black community was measured more in terms of civil rights and black power, movements energized by a growing consciousness of racial injustice at home and changing events around the world.

As Americans who had served admirably in wartime, African Americans may have aspired to the economic progress enjoyed by their white counterparts, however, their yearnings post-World War II reflected more ongoing and basic psychological needs, the actualization of which would dramatically alter the racial scene in the United States and beyond. Cyprian Davis has described the collective turn in black perspective in this manner:

> After the Second World War the United States confronted once again the issue of racial segregation. This time, however, things were different. American society was now forced to confront a new determination and resolve among black Americans. This confrontation now took place in a world in which colonialism was dying and new nations were arising amid wars of liberation. In America it was the beginning of a social revolution that would have enormous – indeed revolutionary – consequences in all sectors of American society.[14]

Historian Peniel Joseph provides additional range to this 1950-60s worldview and sense of self-determination that was emerging among African Americans. According to Joseph,

> Both civil rights and Black Power have immediate roots in the Great Depression and Second World War. If World War II signaled the defeat of fascism and the decline of European colonial empires as the United States also extended new freedoms to far corners of the globe, it also imbued black U.S. veterans and ordinary citizens with a sense of hard-fought political entitlements. Black Americans were among the fiercest partisans in efforts to harness the political energies unleashed during wartime so

---

[14] Davis, O.S.B., Cyprian, *The History of Black Catholics in the United States* (*New* York: Crossroads Publishing, 1991), 255.

as to secure new rights at home as well as abroad.[15]

If much of the developed world was in flux by the mid to late 1950s, the Black community was in a particular flux contending with the general societal, political and economic development issues of the day and times and enduring cultural issues of liberation, equality and self-identity.

Despite the challenges of living black and largely segregated, images of "Negro" aspirations and yearnings were gaining mass attention and blacks were making their mark on U.S. culture.[16] In 1950 Chicagoan Gwendolyn Brooks won the Pulitzer Prize for poetry; Ralph Bunche, a civil rights leader, was awarded the Nobel Peace Prize for mediating Middle East peace between the Arabs and Israelis; the National Basketball Association (NBA) recruited its first three black players; Ethel Waters became the first African American network television star; and author Ralph Ellison's *Invisible Man* was published. In that same year Dr. Kenneth Clark, an African American psychologist, presented the results of his experiments with sixteen black children, ages six to nine, who were interviewed using black and white dolls. The findings of Clark's investigation validated the negative effects of segregation.[17] In 1951, the Pan-American Congress of Pharmacists adopted as its patron a black man, Martin de Porres, a lay brother of the Dominican Order who lived in Peru in the late 16th and early 17th centuries. Martin de Porres was beatified in 1837.[18] Harry Moore, a Florida

---

[15] Peniel E. Joseph, *Dark Days, Bright Nights: From Black Power to Barack Obama* (New York: Basic Civitas Books, 2010), 13-14. Although the U.S. civil rights movement is relatively well-documented in American history, Peniel writes in important detail about the black power movement that has also significantly contributed to the history of Black Americans.

[16] Unless otherwise noted, the Black historical facts are listed by year in Quintard Taylor, *America I Am Black Facts: The Timelines of African American History, 1601-2008* (Carlsbad: SmileyBooks 2009), 149-57.

[17] Juan Williams, *Eyes on the Prize: America's Civil Rights Years 1954-1965,* New York: Penguin Books (1987), 20-21.

[18] Claire Huchet Bishop, *Martín de Porres, Hero,* Boston: Houghton Mifflin Company (1954), 118. As a lay Dominican brother, Blessed Martin (1579-1639) ministered to the poor and sick with prayer, healing medical procedures, and remedial potions and drugs that he mixed

NAACP official, was killed in a bombing on Christmas Day 1951.

Charlotta Bass, a Los Angeles newswoman, was nominated vice-president on the Progressive Party ticket at the 1952 presidential convention. Paul Robeson placed her name in nomination; W.E. B. DuBois seconded the nomination. In the same year, Detroit's Cora Brown was the first black woman elected to the Michigan State Senate. For the first time in seventy-seven years of record-keeping, the Tuskegee Institute reported no lynchings in the United States.

Racial discrimination and segregation persisted through the decade as Black leaders fought for equality in housing, voting rights, education and employment. The 1954 *Brown v. the Board of Education* decision by the U.S. Supreme Court ruled that segregation in public schools was unconstitutional, reversing the judicial doctrine of "separate but equal." In that same year Benjamin. O. Davis, Jr. was appointed the first Black Air Force general and Malcolm X became minister of a Nation of Islam Harlem Temple.

The drama of the Black struggle was prominently featured in several U.S. civil rights actions, including the first organized bus boycott in 1953 in Baton Rouge, the arrests in Montgomery of fifteen-year-old Claudette Colvin and then Rosa Parks for refusing to give up their respective seats on the bus to white riders, and the subsequent 1955 Montgomery bus boycott that propelled Dr. Martin Luther King, Jr. into leadership. Fourteen-year-old Emmitt Till of Chicago was lynched in 1955 during a visit with family in Mississippi. The U.S. Supreme Court issued a ruling known as Brown II ordering that school desegregation proceed with "all deliberate speed." In 1956, as Black students began to register in formerly segregated public schools, violence broke out in communities throughout the South.

In the entertainment arena, Dorothy Dandridge made the cover of *Life Magazine* in 1954, the first African American to be so prominently featured. In 1956, Nat King Cole became the

---

himself. He spent 45 years in the Convent of the Holy Rosary in Lima, Peru as a humble servant to all – human and animal - in need. See also, "St. Martin de Porres: Model of Heroic Charity" in *The Pope Speaks Magazine,* 8 (1962), 49-57.

first African American male to emcee his own prime-time variety show on network television. That same year, Clarence-Rufus Joseph Rivers, a black Catholic priest who dedicated himself to the development of an African American Catholic liturgical aesthetic, was ordained in Cincinnati.[19]

In 1957, Althea Gibson became the first African American winner in the Singles Division of the British Tennis Championship at Wimbledon. Dorothy Height assumed leadership of the National Council of Negro Women, a position she would hold for the next forty-one years.

There was historic movement on the government front:

> Congress passes the Civil Rights Act of 1957, the first legislation protecting black rights since Reconstruction. The act establishes the Civil Rights section of the Justice Department and empowers federal prosecutors to obtain court injunctions against interference with the right to vote. It also creates the federal Civil Rights Commission, with the authority to investigate discriminatory conditions and recommend corrective measures.[20]

Later in the year, President Dwight Eisenhower was compelled to dispatch federal troops to Little Rock to enforce a federal court order to desegregate Central High and protect nine African American students who enrolled as a result of the order. The federal troops would remain at Central High for the remainder of the school year. 30,000 citizens assembled at the Lincoln

---

[19] Clarence-Rufus J. Rivers, "Freeing the Spirit: Very Personal Reflections on One Man's Search for the Spirit in Worship", *U.S. Catholic Historian*, 19 (Spring 2001), 97. Rivers' priestly vocation was one among many that were answered in the mid twentieth century. According to Dolan, "The amount of black priests increased during the period. Up to 1926, only ten American blacks were ordained priests; from 1930 to 1960, 113 were ordained, eighty-three of whom were associated with religious communities." Jay Dolan, ed., 144. The Catholic African World Network 2005 posting on the National Black Catholic Congress website accounts for 250 African American priests and 300 African American sisters in the United States. "Black Catholics: Worldwide Count", National Black Catholic Congress, 2005, http://www.nbccongress.org/black-catholics/worldwide-count-black-catholics-01.asp (accessed August 14, 2014).

[20] Taylor, 153.

Memorial in Washington, D.C. for a Prayer Pilgrimage for Freedom to advocate for desegregation and voter's rights.[21]

The Alvin Ailey Dance Theatre was launched in New York in 1958. In that same year in Atlanta, the Southern Christian Leadership Conference (SCLC) was established; Dr. Martin Luther King, Jr. was the first president. WNTA-TV in New York City hired Louis Lomax, the first African American newscaster. Also in 1958, Cardinal Roncalli was elected Pope John XXIII. By 1959, the ultraconservative Republican Senator Barry Goldwater was the most popular figure invited to speak on U.S. campuses; Malcolm X was number two.[22]

As the decade of the 1950s closed, there continued to be forward motion, relapse, and stalls in African American movement towards the achievement of full and equal civil rights. In 1959, Barry Gordy founded Motown[23] and Lorraine Hansberry's "A Raisin in the Sun", starring Sidney Poitier, opened on Broadway. Ella Fitzgerald and Count Basie won two awards each at the first Grammy Awards Show. Mack Charles Parker was lynched in Mississippi.

The Student Non-Violent Coordinating Committee (SNCC) was formed in 1960 in North Carolina; North Carolina A&T students staged a sit-in at a Woolworth's Drug Store to protest the ban on service to African Americans. At the Olympic Games, Wilma Rudolph won three gold medals in track. President Eisenhower signed the Civil Rights Bill of 1960 to protect voting

---

[21]Clayborne Carson, primary consultant, *Civil Rights Chronicle: The African American Struggle for Freedom,* (Lincolnwood: Publications, International, Ltd., 2003), 148.

[22] Ibid, 111.

[23] "As the great voices grew louder, stronger and multiplied, Motown Records created an outlet where the *truth* (italics provided) could be expressed in an uncensored and enlightened setting. The launch of the Black Forum label was a platform where many of the days' thought leaders could express an Afro-American viewpoint on issues of race, culture and conflict – sentiments that would ultimately emerge in popular music." Taken from "Black Forum: 1960-1972", *Motown: Truth is a Hit,* exhibit at Schomberg Center for Research in Black Culture, Harlem: New York Public Library (February 1-July 26, 2014), visited July 18, 2014.

rights. John F. Kennedy won the presidency of the United States with many African American votes.

Between January and December 1960, seventeen sub-Saharan African nations gained independence from European colonial powers.[24] Government brutality against Black freedom fighters resulted in the 1960 Sharpeville Massacre that sparked worldwide outrage against South African apartheid.[25]

The Congress of Racial Equality (CORE) organized Freedom Rides throughout the Deep South in 1961. The DuSable Museum of African American History, one of the first major museums devoted to Black life in the U.S., was founded in Chicago. In Zaire, the conference of Catholic bishops boldly called for "a locally oriented liturgical movement".[26] On October 1, 1962 James Meredith enrolled in the University of Mississippi, the school's first African American student. Meredith was

---

[24] John Lewis, *Walking with the Wind: A Memoir of the Movement* (San Diego: Harcourt Brace & Company 1998), 71. He asserts, "Zaire, Somalia, Nigeria, the Congo – freedom was stirring in all these places, and we couldn't help being thrilled. Thrilled, but also a little bit ashamed. Here were black people thousands of miles away achieving liberation and independence from nations that had ruled them for centuries, and we still didn't have those rights in a country that was supposed to be free. Black Africans on their native continent were raising their own national flags for the first time in history, and we could not even get a hamburger and a Coke at a soda fountain." Joseph, 49-63, highlights the importance of pan-African consciousness to the U.S. black liberation struggle. During the 1955 Afro-Asian Conference in Bandung, Indonesia, participants discussed concepts of self-rule, Third World solidarity and self-determination. Although he was not in attendance, Malcolm X endorsed the Conference philosophy and eventually rolled those ideas into his own activist message. Harlem, N.Y. became an important U.S. center of Pan African political thought and action promoted by social activists and artists of the day like Lorraine Hansberry, Maya Angelou, and James Baldwin. Cecilia Moore in "Keeping Harlem Catholic: African Catholics and Harlem, 1920-1960", *American Catholic Studies,* 114 (2003): 16-21, counts Black Catholics Billie Holiday, Ellen Tarry and Mary Lou Williams among important activist artists in the 1950-60s Harlem community.

[25] Kevin Shillington, *History of Africa* (New York: St. Martin's Press 1989), 405-6.

[26] Nwaka Chris Egbulem, *The Power of Africentric Celebrations: Inspirations from the Zairean Liturgy* (New York: Crossroad Herder Books, 1996), 33-4.

escorted to class by U.S. marshals and federals troops were dispatched to prevent violent protests.

Of course, history does not happen in discrete moments along a timeline. Every important event unfolds against a complex backdrop of contributing primary and secondary circumstances and causes. Involved in that background is a network of people, most of whom remain nameless. As myriad events of the mid-twentieth century evolved, the profile of black America broadened and became more diversified just as new ideas, capabilities and media images of the times radicalized societies around the world. Political and social unrest, heightened by the prospect of nuclear war that could annihilate the earth in a moment's time, contributed to the instability of people's core beliefs and traditions. Novel concepts and attitudes pushed against established norms, values and expectations. As was typical in many cultural groups, African American youth and college students experimented with fresh interpretations of black consciousness articulated rather stridently in the music, dance, dress, gesture and literature of the day. Some found these modern trends outrageous. On the other hand, elders who welcomed the opportunity at last to express their African identity often embarrassed younger, more conservative, family and church members with their liberated behaviors. At the midpoint of the 20th century, generations had begun to engage in the collective work of reconciling a traditional African heritage with an innovating American culture, a work that would eventually flow over into every aspect of African American life. These negotiations were conducted across class, regional, denominational, generational, political party and ideological lines. Reflecting on this experience from the Black Catholic perspective, Father Joseph M. Davis, S.M. and Brother Cyprian L. Rowe, FMS contended,

> Between the mid-1950s and the late 1960s the remarkable metamorphosis which happened was the strengthening of relational bonds, the reappropriation of cultural identity and pride, and the realization that power is as much a matter of internal disposition as it is an external condition. Within a span of ten years, Negroes became the Black community, moving from legal and persuasive efforts to dismantle desegregation to

non-violent resistance to Black pride, power and nationalism.[27]

From its earliest days in America, a vibrant Black Catholic community had stubbornly rooted itself in the life of the universal Church presented as a predominantly European and European American reality. The struggle of this particular people of God to live free with humanity and faith intact is exemplified in this review of the years from 1950 through the 1960s presented here. What Catholic historian Katrina Sanders says about Black Catholic male leadership can be said of the women religious and the Black Catholic community at-large. According to Sanders: "(a)lthough records of their efforts are invisible in civil rights histories, black Catholic clergy and religious did play a significant role in securing civil rights in their communities. Either covertly or overtly, cautiously or loudly, black Catholic clergy and religious contributed as needed to securing rights for members of their communities in the rural South and the urban North."[28]

The landmarks in U.S. and world events involving Black people presented in this work give just a hint of the audacious and faithful spirit that God has placed in his Black people, a spirit that challenged, animated, comforted and guided them forward through turbulent years of recent U.S. history and braced them for what was to come in the fiery years of the 1960s. These historic touchstones also provide valuable context for John XXIII's decision to convene the Second Vatican Council that opened on October 11, 1962.

---

[27]Davis, S.M., Joseph M. and Cyprian Rowe, F.M.S., "The Development of the National Office for Black Catholics," *U.S. Catholic Historian*, 7 (1988): 265.

[28]Katrina M. Sanders, "Black Catholic Clergy and the Struggle for Civil Rights: Winds of Change," in *Uncommon Faithfulness: The Black Catholic Experience,* eds. M. Shawn Copeland, LaReine-Marie Mosely, and Albert J. Raboteau (Maryknoll: Orbis Books 2009), 79. In this essay, Sanders highlights the civil rights leadership of Fr. August L. Thompson who was ordained in 1957 for the small Louisiana Diocese of Alexandria and the black empowerment ministry of Fr. George Clements, also ordained in 1957, in urban Chicago.

Vatican II and the Black Community

In his reading of the times,

...Pope John intuited that there was something profoundly out of sync in the inner life of the Church: intellectually sterile, liturgically lifeless, moral instruction depending more on imperatives than on invitations, fear emphasized over hope, a clergy cut off from the laity...the Living Word of Scripture all but forgotten, Jesus himself on the margin of piety.[29]

Not only was the Catholic Church of the mid-20th century out of sync internally, the institution was out of step with the modern world undergoing a period of great cultural upheaval and social unrest.[30] His entire life and vocation gave John XXIII broad, sweeping vision of the world as an ecumenical community, yet he moved among the people of God with feet solidly on the ground, ministering with competence, warmth and a simple sophistication. Given his career involvement in international affairs, the prevalence of television as a communications and the inspiration of the Holy Spirit, he surely had his eye on events in the 1950s and early 60s surrounding God's black children throughout the world in the months of preparation for the Council.

Signs of the Times Pointing to the Second Vatican Council

Pope John XXII's actions demonstrated that he was aware

---

[29] Carroll, 17.

[30] For perspectives of the cultural and ecclesial turmoil in U.S. parishes, see in Jay Dolan, ed., *A History from 1850 to the Present: The American Catholic Parish, Volume 1: Thee Northeast, Southeast and South Central States*: Joseph J. Casino, "Part One: From Sanctuary to Involvement: A History of the Catholic Parish in the Northeast, 73-101; Michael J. McNally, "A Peculiar Institution: A History of Catholic Parish Life in the Southwest (1850-1980), 155-217; Charles Nolan, "Modest and Humble Crosses: A History of Catholic Parishes in the South Central Region"292-310. Cecilia A. Moore reports on a local diocesan experience in "Dealing with Desegregation: Black and White Responses to the Desegregation of the Diocese of Raleigh, North Carolina, 1953" in *Uncommon Faithfulness: The Black Catholic Experience*, eds. M. Shawn Copeland, LaReine-Marie Mosely, and Albert J. Raboteau (Maryknoll: Orbis Books 2009), 63-75.

of and concerned with the anxieties and experiences of Catholics of African descent around the world. On May 6, 1962, he canonized Martin de Porres (1579-1639) of Lima, Peru, the lay Dominican brother of Black heritage who was beatified in 1837.[31] He elected Laurean Rugambwa (1912-1997) of Tanzania the first African Cardinal in March 1960. The Pope mentioned the elevation of Rugambwa as evidence of the continent's long and enduring connection with the Church in a radio message delivered to African Catholics on June 5, 1960.[32] His encyclicals, propagated between 1959 and 1963, critiqued the abuses of modernization and prescribed spiritual and social justice remedies for war, injustice, inequality and poverty, situations that plagued Black American and African communities. Surely God's Black people were of consequence to this pope.

John XXIII convened the Second Vatican Council in 1962, inviting bishops of the church from all over the world to reflect and consult, pray and discuss contemporary life in the light of

---

[31] See *The Pope Speaks Magazine,* 8 (1962), "St. Martin de Porres: Model of Heroic Charity" and "The Canonization of a Saint, 91-95. In a May 1962 address to cardinals, bishops, clergy and laity assembled for the celebration to canonize Martin de Porres, John XXIII speaks of the new saint: "As we stated at the beginning of Our sermon, We feel that it is a most happy coincidence that, in the course of this year in which We decreed the celebration of the Ecumenical Council, the honors of sainthood should be bestowed upon Martin de Porres. This, because the pinnacles of Christian holiness which he attained, and the splendor of dazzling virtue, of which his whole life shone as an example, are of such magnitude that we may view in him, as it were, the wholesome fruits which We most ardently desire from this forthcoming and most solemn event, both for the Church and for the entire human community.", "St. Martin de Porres", 55.

[32] See "Radiomensaje del Papa Juan XXIII a los Católicos Africanos", Domingo 5 de Junio de 1960, http://www.vatican.va/holy father//john xxiii/messages/pont message s/1960/documents/hf j-xxiii mes 19600605 fedeli-africa sp.html (accessed August 14, 2014). Speaking familiarly in Spanish to African Catholics, particularly the faithful in recently liberated African nations and those in the struggle for liberation, Pope John XXIII acknowledged the rich spirituality of the people and recognized the timeless presence of Africa in the history of the Church. He offered examples, contemporary and ancient, of African faithful, martyrs and clergy who have witnessed wholeheartedly to the faith.

Catholic teaching.[33] Although he died the following year, the Council continued through 1965 under the leadership of his successor, Pope Paul VI.[34]

"Vatican Council II met in the great nave of St. Peter's Basilica in Rome in four sessions in the autumns of the years 1962 to 1965, with committees doing extensive work between sessions. Made up of about 2,400 bishops, with about 500 *periti*, or experts, and something between 50 and 200 "observers" and "auditors" in attendance, the Council issued sixteen distinct statements..."[35] The aims of the Council were introduced in *Sacrosanctum Concilium* (The Constitution on the Sacred Liturgy), the first conciliar document promulgated in 1963. *Sacrosanctum Concilium* was intended to invigorate the Christian life of the faithful, to adapt institutions to the needs of the times, to foster unity among those who believe in Christ and to call all of humanity into communion with the Church.[36]

The attention of the Black Catholic community was not fixed on the extensive preparations for and dramatic opening of the Council. It was concentrated instead on the daily dramas associated with the fight for freedom, dignity and full Black personhood in the many situations where all that was at risk. As a result of their history and contemporary circumstances, Black Catholics were dedicated, invigorated Christian disciples.

---

[33] A total of two hundred ninety-six bishops and other prelates from Africa attended Vatican Council II, there were three hundred from Asia, four hundred eighty-nine from South America, eighty-four representing Central America and four hundred four from North America. Huebsch, *Vatican II in Plain English: The Council*, 165-6. Bishop Harold Robert Perry (1916-1991), was the first self-identified African American ordained a Catholic bishop. Appointed on September 29, 1965 Auxiliary Bishop of New Orleans, Perry attended the fourth and final session of Vatican Council II, September to December 1965. *"Second Vatican Council Session Four Council Fathers"*, May 2014, http://www.catholic-hierarchy.org/event/ecv2-4-10.html (accessed August 4, 2014), 3.

[34] *The Faithful Revolution: Vatican II,* (Cincinnati: RCL Benzinger, 1997), a 5-part documentary DVD set, gives a brilliant historical overview of the Council and its implementation in the Church of the United States.

[35] Carroll, 15.

[36] *Sacrosanctum Concilium, Vatican Council II: The Conciliar and Post Conciliar Documents,* ed. Austin Flannery, O.P., (Boston: Daughters of St. Paul, 1988 rev.), #1, 1.

They could sense a fundamental disconnect between the workings of the institutional Church and their everyday state of affairs. Despite the political status quo and because of a deep faith in God, they trusted that all who believe in Christ Jesus (and good folk who do not) would someday come together to promote God's reign on earth. Although they may not have been fully tuned in to the ceremony and proceedings, the simply stated aims of Vatican Council II resonated with the spirit of Black Catholic faithful. The fulfillment of those conciliar aims continues even until today as the Body of Christ strives to discern their meanings in a new age.

Signs of the Times: Black Catholic Initiatives in Liturgical Renewal

M. Shawn Copeland's analysis of the relevance of Vatican II for the faithful and the whole people of God is useful here. Copeland contends,

> From its earliest sessions, the Second Vatican Council turned the mind and heart of the Church toward the concrete social (i.e., political, economic, and technological) world, and, the pastoral constitution, "The Church in the Modern World," identified itself with it.[37] The sixteen documents promulgated by the Council treated the theological understandings of the nature and the mission of the Church, its relation to Judaism, and to other world religions; restored to public view Catholic respect for individual conscience; advocated the notion of religious freedom; examined the roots of modern atheism...The Council also engaged the grave problems of the time – the economic and political exploitation of peoples and nations of the third world, the threat of world destruction by nuclear war, disregard for the sanctity of human life, racism and unbridled technological innovation. The Second Vatican Council rethought the notion of spirituality and holiness of life, asserting that all Christians are called to holiness and encouraging the laity to more active involvement in the apostolic mission of the Church. Insisting the lay women and men have a

---

[37] Flannery, *Documents of Vatican II*, *Gaudium et Spes*.

"special and indispensable role in the mission of the Church, "the Council reminded the hierarchy and clergy that the laity must not be deprived of "their rightful freedom to act on their own initiative."[38]

By the 1950s important reforms in liturgy and scripture, the discussion of which began early in the twentieth century, had found good soil in Catholic theological and pastoral settings throughout the world. So that on the second day of Vatican II, October 16, 1962, the Council Fathers could easily agree to take on reform of the liturgy as its first task. Liturgical renewal was a topic uppermost on the Council agendas of many of the bishops assembled due to the experimentation and discussions on the topic already underway in Catholic faith communities, particularly in the Church in the first world. The preparation for the discussion had been prepared by a sizeable committee of pastoral and liturgical experts.[39] Vatican II historian Bill Huebsch outlined the manner in which the Council approached this matter:

> October 22, 1962: The **schema** (draft document) **on Liturgy is introduced** for debate. The press office reports that this is the first topic because the Council's work will be directed primarily towards the task of the internal renewal of the Church. The debate is wide-ranging, including suggestions for use of the vernacular, more varied use of Scripture, communion under both forms, and concelebration. The discussion on the Liturgy lasts through fifteen general sessions, ending on November 13. The council fathers propose 625 amendments to the original schema. It eventually meets with their overwhelming approval, a blow for the conservatives at the council.[40]

---

[38] Copeland, "A Cadre of Women Religious", 125; Flannery, *Documents of Vatican II, Lumen Gentium,* Ch. IV; see also *Apostolicam Actuositatem,* #1, #24.

[39] Bill Huebsch, *Vatican II in Plain English, The Constitutions* (Allen: Thomas More, 1997), 89-93; Edward P. Hahnenberg, "Documents: Prefatory Material" in *Vatican II: The Essential Texts* (New York: Image Books, 2012), 29-33.

[40] Huebsch, *Vatican II in Plain English: The Council,* 110. (emphasis in the original)

Pope Paul VI promulgated the "Constitution on the Sacred Liturgy" on December 4, 1963. An essential passage of the document stated:

> Mother Church earnestly desires that all the faithful should be led to that fully conscious, and active participation in liturgical celebrations which is demanded by the very nature of the liturgy Such participation by the Christian people as "a chosen race, a royal priesthood, a holy nation, a redeemed people (1 Pet. 2:9; cf. 2:4-5), is their right and duty by reason of their baptism.
>
> In the restoration and promotion of the sacred liturgy, this full and active participation by all the people is the aim to be considered before all else; for it is the primary and indispensable source from which the faithful are to derive the true Christian spirit; and therefore pastors of souls must zealously strive to achieve it, by means of the necessary instruction, in all their pastoral work (14).

The following section will lift up two examples of Black Catholic creativity that 1) were factors in pre-Vatican Council II liturgical reform, 2) were spurred on by the pervasive cultural unrest that characterized the 1950s and 1960s, 3) embraced the spirit of Vatican II renewal and 4) continue to influence contemporary Catholic liturgy. In their distinct contexts the Zairean Bishops' Conference in Central Africa and Father Clarence Joseph Rivers in Cincinnati, Ohio had wrestled with what some believed were incompatible actualities: black culture and the Catholic faith. The folk with whom they ministered were engrossed to varying degrees in a changing self-awareness of Blackness that impacted nearly every aspect of human existence, including their faith life. Long before the Council assembled, these prophetic pastors had begun working towards the key principle promoted in the *Constitution on the Sacred Liturgy:* "(t)he Church earnestly desires that all the faithful be led to that full, conscious, and active participation in liturgical celebrations called for by the very nature of the liturgy. . . In the reform and promotion of the liturgy, this full and active participation by all the people is the aim to be considered before all else. For it is the primary and indispensable source from which the faithful are to derive the true Christian spirit . . ."[41]

The Zairean Mass

Sacramental theologian Nwaka Chris Egbulem suggests that "(t)he Church of Zaire was the first truly to address the issue of bringing African life and sense into Catholic liturgy."[42] Formerly known as Belgium Congo, the country of Zaire won its political independence in June 1960. At the time, Zaire (now the Democratic Republic of the Congo) was a nation of more than fifty three million people and two hundred plus ethnic groups that spoke Tshiluba, Swahili, Lingala, Kikongo and French. Half the population was Catholic; Belgium Congo had been evangelized primarily by Italian and Portuguese missionaries. The Catholic University of Kinshasha (the Lovanium), founded in 1954 and patterned after the University of Louvain in Belgium, was the first Catholic university in Africa. The Zairean episcopal conference also established a theology faculty in 1957 "given the mission of training seminary teachers and lecturers for higher institutes of learning. It is a faculty committed to research and reflection on African Christianity".[43] The investment in these scholarly resources - theological, philosophical, anthropological and liturgical – corresponded with the faithful's demand for a Catholic way of life more authentically rooted in Zairean culture and proved to be a catalyst for local church reform confirmed by Vatican Council II.[44]

The bishops of Zaire recognized the need to incorporate aspects of African culture into Catholic worship. An early experiment in liturgical reform was "the "Missa Luba", a humble but daring attempt to use African musical instruments to

---

[41] *Sancrosanctum Concilium,* 14.

[42] Egbulem, 33.

[43] Elochukwu E. Uzukwu, *Worship as Body Language: Introduction to Christian Worship: An African Orientation,* (Collegeville: The Liturgical Press, 1997), 298. Uzukwu, a scripture and liturgical scholar, provides essential foundation for the study and implementation of liturgical inculturation affirmed in theory in Vatican Council II.

[44] Ibid, 298.

accompany the Roman Mass sung in Latin. At the time of its release in the early 1960s, it was the first introduction of African rhythm, drums, and gongs into Catholic celebrations."[45] Aware of a general push for liturgical reform in the universal church, the bishops in a 1961 national meeting identified the following "adaptations" required to update the Mass in Zaire: use of the vernacular, incorporation of local expressions and cultural communication styles, African prayers and revised rituals, in essence, an African-styled Mass.

Vatican Council II responded in some ways to the Conference's requests for liturgical reforms better suited to the needs and genius of the Zairean people of God. However, as a result of their intense and early advocacy, their commitment to African cultural research and consistent consultation with Rome, the bishops of Zaire managed to lead the effort to "create a liturgy that incarnates the message of revelation in a specific socio-cultural context, thus presenting the mystery celebrated by the Christian community in an expressive and comprehensive manner. It was not enough for the liturgy to be Zairean, it must also be Christian."[46] Pressing the renewals of Vatican Council II in accordance with the prescriptions of the Vatican Congregation for Divine Worship, the "Missel Romain pour les Dioceses du Zaire (Roman Missal for the Diocese of Zaire, popularly known as the "Rite Zairois (Zairean Rite) was officially approved on April 30, 1988.[47]

> Even in the liturgy the Church has no wish to impose a rigid uniformity...Rather does she respect and foster the qualities and talents of the various races and nations. Anything in these people's way of life which is not indissolubly bound up with superstition and error she studies with sympathy, and if possible, preserves intact. She sometimes even admits such things into the liturgy itself, provided they harmonize with its true and authentic

---

[45] Egbulem, 35.

[46] Ibid, 36.

[47] Ibid, 47. Egbulem's depth of research and detail in this report on the evolution of the Zairean liturgy conveys important understanding of the process of liturgical inculturation the need for which is ongoing in the life of the church.

spirit. Provided that the substantial unity of the Roman rite is preserved, provision shall be made, when revising the liturgical books, for legitimate variations and adaptations to different groups, regions and peoples...This should be borne in mind when drawing up the rites and determining rubrics.[48]

The visionary leadership of the conference of Zairean bishops is well reflected in this selection from the "Constitution on the Sacred Liturgy" in which the church once again affirmed in concept the cultural, ethnic and national diversity of God's people and acknowledged the role of culture in Catholic worship. In the U.S. Catholic Church, pre-Vatican II grassroots efforts at updating Sunday worship in response to the particular cultural needs and gifts of the people were also underway. A homegrown African American Catholic virtuoso – liturgist, composer, musician, and artist – had entered the scene.

Fr. Clarence Rufus Joseph Rivers: Black Priest-Artist

Born in Selma, Alabama in September 1931, Rivers moved as a child with his family to Cincinnati. He studied in local Catholic schools. His deep interest in the priesthood was encouraged and Clarence Rufus attended a diocesan seminary.[49] Upon ordination in 1956, Fr. Rivers was assigned to St. Joseph's parish in Cincinnati's West End where he ministered with Msgr. Clement Busemeyer. Reflecting on this experience, Rivers said, "I expected this exteriorly gruff, teutonic pastor to be unconcerned about the *quality* of worship; his masses took from twenty to thirty minutes, the "sacred words" slovenly raced over in the widespread custom of the day. However, he was very much concerned that worship was not reaching and touching the people in the pews."[50]

Although his own style of presiding at Mass did not reflect his concern, Busemeyer provided the professional support and space for the novice Fr. Rivers to try different approaches to

---

[48] *Sacrosanctum Concilium,* #37-8.

[49] Clarence Joseph Rivers, "No Prejudice in Seminary, Writes Negro," *The Catholic Telegraph (*July 8, 1949).

[50] Rivers, "Freeing the Spirit", 97.

bring about an everyday change in the assembly's liturgical experience. Rivers recalled:

> In presiding at Mass, usually the main parish Mass, I would intensify my efforts to read the Latin texts so as to convey their meaning. There was no illusion that the people would understand the Latin, but they must see that I, for the most part, did understand and was more or less raptured by my understanding. There was a certain validity in presuming that they could be moved by experiencing that I was moved. However, they must understand their own responses, and they must convey the meaning in the English hymns, psalms, and songs, to themselves and to one another. That was not to ask a great deal for the moment, and it laid a basis for further development."[51]

One further development in Rivers' repertoire was the incorporation of Black music in Catholic worship. His own first composition, "God is Love" and a recorded copy of the Zairean "*Missa Luba*" gave him and his collaborators, the Sisters of St. Francis (Oldenburg) on staff at the parish elementary school, the resources to teach the St. Joseph student body, and then the St. Joseph Sunday assembly, new music that boldly invigorated the celebration of the Roman Mass. As his appreciation for Black culture in Catholic worship deepened, Rivers worked to develop his preaching style. And he spent time before the start of the main Sunday Mass prepping the congregation to sing well to enhance, all the more, their "full, conscious and active" involvement in the liturgical enterprise. He describes the experimentation: "The sisters and I were products of our time. Therefore, we did not think of our attempts in worship as revolutionary; rather we were attempting to recapture what we thought was a forgotten tradition. We were full-time teachers who worked on worship – mainly on music and congregational participation – only in a "beginning way".[52] Their "beginning way" in pre-Vatican Council II

---

[51] Ibid, 98.
[52] Ibid, 103.

Cincinnati, led to a realization that would motivate a full-blown African American Catholic liturgical movement:

> ...that all drama, including the drama of worship, needed movement from beginning to middle to end...It slowly dawned on me that a well-structured (aesthetically structured) worship was the same as a vitally effective, spiritually moving worship...St. Joseph's parish was moving with moderate speed toward an effective worship and a more comprehensive idea of inculturation, i.e. synthesizing and integrating African American culture and Catholic worship. This was a matter more sophisticated than adding a few Black-flavored hymns/songs onto an otherwise unyielding Roman rite.[53]

Although he went on to produce classic works and make singular contributions to the development of a contemporary liturgical movement in the United States[54], Rivers' pastoral intuitions as a new priest established important ecclesial values in the 1950s and 60s - respect for the cultural genius of a people, a passion for "full, conscious and active" worship, collaboration in ministry and practiced excellence in liturgical performance in service to the people of God – that were reinforced in Vatican Council II.

These are brief illustrations of Black Catholics who, in the midst of the cultural revolutions of the mid-twentieth century, engaged in church reforms in their local situations that led to the call for Vatican II. Many Black Catholic developments incubated during the late 1950s and early 1960s, encouraged by these and other cultural initiatives. For example, there was a growing community of Black Catholic religious and clergy who faced questions, concerns and challenges related to Black identity and Roman Catholic vocation in their various ministry

---

[53] Ibid, 101.

[54] See Clarence Rivers, "The Oral African Tradition Versus the Ocular Western Tradition", *This Far by Faith: American Black Worship and Its African Roots* (Washington: National Office for Black Catholics and Liturgical Conference, 1976), 38-49; Rivers, *The Spirit in Worship* (Cincinnati: Stimuli, Inc., 1978) and Mary E. McGann, RSCJ, "*Let It Shine*": *The Emergence of African American Catholic Worship* (New York: Fordham University Press, 2008).

settings. Also underway was a slow shift in Black Catholic consciousness that took into consideration the particular struggles, gifts and needs of the community and began to speak to the stark incompatibility of social segregation and injustice with the Gospel preached by the Church. Fresh, young African American Catholic scholars were exploring black approaches to theology, catechetics, ethics, liturgy and pastoral ministry. They were backed by a corps of accomplished liturgical musicians who experimented with the treasury of traditional Black music in the context of Catholic liturgy. As they matured, many of these fledgling efforts responded to the needs of Black Christian disciples while reinforcing Vatican II values, reconciling work that continued in the decades that followed, even until today.

Clearly, the Good News proclaimed in those Fall gatherings of the Council fifty years ago and the conciliar documents themselves still speak to the particular situations – of blood, sweat and tears - that Black people in the U.S. (and Africa) faced in that era. Their yearnings, aspirations and the dramatic features of the segregated, yet-to-be-liberated world in which they lived was always the concern of Jesus Christ. In the years preceding the Council, The Church universal was briefed on life in the modern world through technology, the popular movements, social unrest and the prospect of war that hung heavy in the air.[55] African American and African leaders read the signs of the times; they protested, strategized, and advocated for righteousness in the light of the Gospel.

Conclusion

Further investigation and cross study is needed to put a finger on tangible theological, liturgical, social and historical benefits that the Council brings to bear on the development of the post-1960s Black Catholic community. It must be noted that challenges to that faith development presented with a vengeance in the mid-1960s; they included the assassinations of

---

[55]White Catholic reaction to Vatican Council II teachings and the quest for racial justice in the U.S. church are profiled by John T. McGreevy in "Racial Justice and the People of God: The Second Vatican Council, the Civil Rights Movement and American Catholics", *Religion and American Culture: A Journal of Interpretation,* 4 (Summer 1994): 221-254.

national leaders and the continued killing of black children, racism and resistance to black progress, neighborhood violence and riots, and a radicalized self-consciousness that would boldly embrace the values of the Black Nationalism and Black Power movements.

In conclusion, there is evidence that leading up to the Council, Africa was on the mind and heart of Pope John XXIII. It is fair to speculate that he was well aware through the media that a minority of Blacks – mostly professionals, entertainers and athletes - was advancing in American society, gaining limited civil rights, but that the majority of the people were caught in situations of poverty, injustice and lack of opportunity. He assembled Vatican Council II to bring to the Church's attention signs of the times such as these, to consider what must be done in light of the Gospels, church teachings and social justice. The Council represents the type of collaborative effort needed within the Church, with other churches and communities of faith, and organizations of good will to address the cultural mayhem - global and local – that exists even until today and to proclaim Good News to those in need. To conclude, fifty years after its convocation, Vatican Council II is an ongoing movement of God's people whose continuing evolution in Christ is vital for the redemption of the African American community and all the holy people of God.

Works Cited

Bishop, Claire Huchet. *Martín de Porres, Hero*. Boston: Houghton Mifflin Company, 1954.

"Black Catholics: Worldwide Count." National Black Catholic Congress, 2005. <http://www.nbccongress.org/black-catholics/worldwide-count-black-catholics-01.asp> (August 14, 2014).

"Black Forum: 1960-1972." *Motown: Truth is a Hit* Exhibit. (February 1-July 26, 2014). Schomberg Center for Research in Black Culture, Harlem: New York Public Library, (July 18, 2014).

"Canonization of a Saint." *The Pope Speaks Magazine* 8 (1962): 91-5.

Cantwell, Daniel M., ed. *Catholics Speak on Race Relations*. Chicago: Fides Publishers Association, 1952.

Carroll, James. "Introductions: The Beginning of Change." In *Vatican II: The Essential Texts*, edited by Norman Tanner, 14-16. New York: Image Books, 2012.

Casino, Joseph J. "Part One: From Sanctuary to Involvement." In *A History from 1850 to the Present: The American Catholic Parish, Volume 1: The Northeast, Southeast and South Central States*, Jay Nolan, ed. Mahwah: Paulist Press, 1987.

Carson, Clayborne, consultant. *Civil Rights Chronicle: The African-American Struggle for Freedom*. Lincolnwood: Publications International, Ltd., 2003.

Copeland, M. Shawn. "A Cadre of Women Religious Committed to Black Liberation: The National Black Sisters' Conference." *U.S. Catholic Historian* 14 (1996): 121-44.

---. "African American Catholics and Black Theology: An Interpretation." In *African American Religious Studies: An Interdisciplinary Anthology*, edited by Gayraud S. Wilmore, 228-248. Durham: Duke University Press, 1988.

Davis, Cyprian . *The History of Black Catholics in the United States*. New York: Crossroads Publishing, 1991.

Davis, Joseph M. and Cyprian Rowe. "The Development of the National Office for Black Catholics." *U.S. Catholic Historian* (7), 1988: 265-89.

Egbulem, Nwaka Chris. *The Power of Africentric Celebrations: Inspirations from the Zairean Liturgy*. New York: Crossroad Herder Book, 1996.

Flannery, Austin, ed. *Gaudium et Spes*" In Vatican Council II: The Conciliar and Post Conciliar Documents. Boston: Daughters of St. Paul, 1988.

---. *Lumen Gentium* In Vatican Council II: The Conciliar and Post Conciliar Documents. Boston: Daughters of St. Paul, 1988.

---. *Sancrosanctum Concilium* In Vatican Council II: The Conciliar and Post Conciliar Documents. Boston: Daughters of St. Paul, 1988.

Hahnenberg, Edward P. "Documents: Prefatory Material." In *Vatican II: The Essential Texts*. New York: Image Books (2012): 29-33.

Huebsch, Bill. *Vatican II in Plain English: The Constitutions*. Allen: Thomas More Publishing, 1997.

---. *Vatican II in Plain English: The Council*. Allen: Thomas More Publishing, 1997.

Joseph, Peniel E. *Dark Days, Bright Nights: From Black Power to Barack Obama*. New York: Basic Civitas Books, 2010.

Kelly, J.N.D. *The Oxford Dictionary of Popes*, Oxford: Oxford University Press, 2005.

Lewis, John. *Walking with the Wind: A Memoir of the Movement*. San Diego: Harcourt Brace & Company, 1998.

McGann, R.S.C.J., Mary E. *Let It Shine: The Emergence of African American Catholic Worship*. New York: Fordham University Press, 2008.

McGreevy, John T. "Racial Justice and the People of God: The Second Vatican Council, the Civil Rights Movement and American Catholics." *Religion and American Culture: A Journal of Interpretation* 4, no. 2 (Summer 1994): 221-254.

McNally, Michael J. "A Peculiar Institution: A History of Catholic Parish Life in the Southwest (1850-1980)." In A History from 1850 to the Present: The American Catholic Parish, Volume 1: The Northeast, Southeast and South Central States, edited by Jay Dolan. Mahwah: Paulist Press, 1987.

Moore, Cecilia. "Dealing with Desegregation: Black and White Responses to the Desegregation of the Diocese of Raleigh, North Carolina, 1953." In *Uncommon Faithfulness: The Black Catholic Experience,* edited by M. Shawn Copeland, LaReine-Marie Mosely, and Albert J. Raboteau, 63-75. Maryknoll: Orbis Books, 2009.

---. "Keeping Harlem Catholic: African Catholics and Harlem, 1920-1960." *American Catholic Studies* 114 (2003): 3-21.

Nolan, Charles. "Modest and Humble Crosses: A History of Catholic Parishes in the South Central Region." In *A History from 1850 to the Present: The American Catholic Parish, Volume 1: The Northeast, Southeast and South Central States,* edited by Jay Dolan. Mahwah: Paulist Press, 1987.

O'Malley, John W. *A History of the Popes: From Peter to the Present.* Lanham: Rowman and Littlefield Publishers, Inc., 2010.

O'Toole, James M. *The Faithful: A History of Catholics in America.* Cambridge: Belknap Press of Harvard University Press, 2008.

"Pope John XIII's Opening Address to the Second Vatican Council". October 11, 1962. <http://vatican2voice.org/91docs/opening_speech.htm> (accessed July 7, 2014).

"Radiomensaje del Papa Juan XXIII a los Católicos Africanos." Domingo 5 de Junio de 1960. <http://www.vatican.va/holy_father//john_xxiii/messages/pont_messages/1960/documents/hf_j-xxiii_mes_19600605_fedeli-africa_sp.html> (accessed August 14, 2014).

Rivers, Clarence-Rufus J. "Freeing the Spirit: Very Personal Reflections on One Man's Search for the Spirit in Worship." *U.S. Catholic Historian* 19 (Spring 2001): 95-143.

---. "No Prejudice in Seminary, Writes Negro." *The Catholic Telegraph,* July 8, 1949.

---. "The Oral African Tradition Versus the Ocular Western Tradition." *This Far by Faith: American Black Worship and Its African Roots.* Washington: National Office for Black Catholics and Liturgical Conference, 1976.

---. *The Spirit in Worship.* Cincinnati: Stimuli, Inc., 1978.

Rooney, Francis. *The Global Vatican: An Inside Look at the Catholic Church, World Politics and the Extraordinary Relationship Between the United States and the Holy See.* Lanham: Sheed & Ward, 2013.

"St. Martin de Porres: Model of Heroic Charity." *The Pope Speaks Magazine* 8 (1962): 49-57.

Sanders, Katrina M. "Black Catholic Clergy and the Struggle for Civil Rights: Winds of Change." In *Uncommon Faithfulness: The Black Catholic Experience,* edited by M. Shawn Copeland, LaReine-Marie Mosely, and Albert J. Raboteau, 78-93. Maryknoll: Orbis Books, 2009.

"Second Vatican Council Session Four Council Fathers." May 2014. <http://www.catholic-hierarchy.org/event/ecv2-4-10.html> (August 4, 2014).

Shillington, Kevin. *History of Africa.* New York: St. Martin's Press, 1989.

Styles, Eric T. "Clarence Rufus Joseph Rivers." *Liturgical Pioneers, Pastoral Musicians and Liturgists.* November 2008. <http:liturgicalleaders.blogspot.com/2008/11/clarence-rufus-joseph-rivers.html> (accessed July 9, 2014).

Taylor, Quintard. *America I Am Black Facts: The Timelines of African American History, 1601-2008.* Carlsbad: SmileyBooks, 2009.

Uzukwu, Elochukwu E. *Worship as Body Language: Introduction to Christian Worship: An African Orientation.* Collegeville: The Liturgical Press, 1997.

Williams, Juan. *Eyes on the Prize: America's Civil Rights Years 1954-1965.* New York: Penguin Books, 1987.

Immigrants and Cultural Continuance in the Liturgy: Celebrating the Nigerian Igbo Mass in the United States

Sr. M. Reginald Anibueze, DDL
University of Notre Dame
South Bend, Indiana

Abstract: The dynamics of the celebration of the Igbo Mass in the United States reveals a cultural nostalgia inherent among Igbo immigrants, one that aims at preserving the Igbo identity and culture, even in the diaspora. Convinced to maintain their cultural heritage on foreign soil, Nigerian Igbo Catholic immigrants established faith communities where liturgical worship is performed and expressed in ways that are consistent and meaningful to Igbo indigenous ways of worship. This essay studies the liturgical life of Nigerian Igbo Catholics in the United States, and how a people's cultural and religious heritage is preserved, sustained, and promoted in the liturgy. Thus, the celebration of Igbo mass in the United States serves as an avenue for encouraging and fostering a people's cultural heritage for future generations.

Keywords: Igbo, Immigrant, Mass, Nigerian, Culture, Identity, Catholic, Liturgy, Music, Dance, Preaching, Language, Community

Introduction

Nigerians are known to value their ethnicity more than their nationality, and even as migrants, one's ethnicity or tribal affiliation is very apparent in the interactions between Nigerians.[1] Most Nigerian immigrants in the United States are clustered in large urban areas which encourage the creation of ethnic and religious associations where such ties are reinforced. These religious groups serve the Nigerian immigrant community well in maintaining their cultural identities and values.

Convinced of the need to maintain an autonomous cultural expression of faith as well as teach and preserve the Igbo

---

[1] Obiefuna Onwughalu, *Parents' Involvement in Education: The Experience of an African Immigrant Community in Chicago* (Bloomington: iUniverse, Inc.:2011), 25.

language, culture, and tradition, Nigerian Igbo Catholics have found it not just essential but equally pragmatic to establish faith communities wherein worship can offer an indigenous experience since, "a major motivation that spurs immigrants to create or join congregations composed of fellow immigrants is to enjoy the companionship of others who share their ethnic background ... Immigrant religious institutions provide the physical and social spaces in which those who share the same traditions, customs, and languages can reproduce many aspects of their native cultures for themselves and attempt to pass them on to their children."[2] Ethnic communities' desire to be true to their faith and cultural identities is supported in the document *Sacrosanctum Concilium* of the Second Vatican Council.

> Even in the liturgy, the Church has no wish to impose a rigid uniformity in matters which do not implicate the faith or the good of the whole community; rather does she respect and foster the genius and talents of the various races and peoples. Anything in these peoples' way of life which is not indissolubly bound up with superstition and error she studies with sympathy and, if possible, preserves intact. Sometimes in fact she admits such things into the liturgy itself, so long as they harmonize with its true and authentic spirit.[3]

Sacrosanctum Concilium clearly encourages the preservation and incorporation of cultural heritages into the liturgy of through the expression of faith, the celebration of the sacraments and the unity of ministry. Thus, through the Eucharistic liturgy, cultural tradition can be preserved to posterity.

The sense of cultural integrity expressed in the liturgy not only reflects the worshipping community's deep understanding of the Catholic faith, but also aims to bequeath the rich Igbo cultural heritage to posterity who are far removed from the homeland. Indeed the dynamics of the celebration of the Igbo Mass reveals the cultural nostalgia that is inherent in migrant Igbos, one that aims at preserving the Igbo identity and culture,

---

[2] Helen Ebaugh, and Janet Chafetz, *Religion and the New Immigrants* (California: Alta Mira Press, 2000), 385.

[3] *Sacrosanctum Concilium,37.*

even as immigrants. Many adult Igbo Catholics are convinced that their children, born in a foreign land, are bound to lose their identity unless there is concerted effort to impart the Igbo language, custom, and mores, within a liturgical framework. The purpose of this study is to show how a people's rich cultural heritage is expressed, sustained, and preserved in the liturgy using Igbo immigrants in the United States as a case study.

Interestingly, this study was born at a PhD seminar class on Modern Liturgy where I tried to conduct research on the how immigrants preserve their cultural heritage in the Eucharistic liturgy. Being an insider with respect to the Igbo culture, and having experienced firsthand the range of challenging conditions that are met by other Igbo Catholic immigrants in the United States, I was interested in some of the ways Nigerian Igbo Catholics maintain elements of their culture in the Catholic Mass. Since there are very few published resources on Nigerian Igbo Catholics, I used the Igbo Catholic community USA website as a resource,[4] and supplemented it with interviews with members of the community and with participant observation conducted in 2010 at the Igbo Catholic Community Mass in the Archdiocese of Chicago.

Given the need for a sustained cultural identity among the Igbo people on alien soil, this study focuses on the liturgical life of the Nigerian Igbo Catholic community in the United States with a focus on the Mass and on present-day cultural nostalgia inherent among the migrant Igbos. From the data collected and the participant observation, the essay argues that the central concern of forming these faith communities by Igbo migrants in the United States is for the enrichment of their communal life and welfare, reinforcing their cultural identity, and the preservation of their culture and religious heritage on foreign soil. I hope to add to the scholarship of the religious activities of African immigrant communities in the United States.

This study will be divided into four parts; A. The Igbo People of Nigeria, Immigration to the United States and Quest for an Identity; B. Formation of Igbo catholic communities in

---

[4] Igbo Catholic Community- Houston, ICCH, http://www.igbocatholicshouston.org/history.htm [accessed August 9, 2012].

America; C. Incorporation of Igbo Culture and Traditions in the Eucharistic Liturgy; and D. Significance of the Igbo Mass for Immigrants.

A. The Igbo People of Nigeria, Immigration to the United States and Quest for an Identity

Nigeria, one of the largest countries in Africa, is situated on the eastern end of the West Africa region; east of the Republic of Benin, south of the Republic of Niger and Chad, west of Cameroon, and north of the Bight of Benin and Bight of Biafra in the Atlantic Ocean's Gulf of Guinea. In comparative terms, Nigeria is larger than the states of California, Nevada, and Utah combined. It stretches about 767 kilometers (479.375 miles) in its east-west span wide, and about 1,605 kilometers (1,003.125 miles) from north to south.[5] Igbos constitute one of the largest and most populous ethnic groups in Nigeria and in sub-Sahara Africa.[6] With an estimated population of over 30 million people,[7] the Igbo-speaking people are located in south-eastern Nigeria. Igbos are bounded in the east by the Ibibio people, in the north by the Igalla, Idoma and Ogoja people, in the south by the Ijo and in the west by the Edo.

Due to the effects of migration, the Trans-Atlantic slave trade, and the peripatetic nature of Igbos, there are descendant ethnic Igbo populations in other countries within as well as outside Africa. In the twentieth century, the migration of Nigerians to the United States has depended on three factors: 1) a quest for higher education; 2) the Nigerian civil war (1967-1970) and consequent economic instability and unemployment; and 3) military dictatorship and the ensuing effects of political repression.[8] It is estimated that more than one million

---

[5] Kalu Ogbaa, *The Nigerian Americans* (Westport: Greenwood Press, 2003), 4.

[6] Christopher Ejizu, "The Traditional Igbo Perception of Reality: Its Dialectics and Dilemma," *Bigard Theological Studies* 9(1989):58-73.

[7] CIA World Fact Book, Nigeria: https://www.cia.gov/library/publications/the-world-factbook/geos/ni.html (accessed November 18, 2013). This estimate is 18% of the total population (174,507,539) as of July, 2013.

[8] For further information on migration of Igbo people to the United States, see Y.K Djamba, "African Immigrants in the United States: A

Nigerians now reside in the U.S.[9] But, it is quite difficult to determine how many of these Nigerians are Igbo because the U.S. census statistics and those of the United States Citizenship and Immigration Services (USCIS) consider only race and nationality, not ethnicity.[10] Nigerian Igbo immigrants have been drawn mainly to large urban cities, such as; New York, Houston, Los Angeles, Chicago, Dallas, Atlanta, Baltimore, and Washington, D.C. It is in these major urban communities that Igbo liturgical practices thrive today.

The Igbo have been exposed to Christian missionary activity since 1841; in 1857 an Anglican mission was opened at the important town of Onitsha along the Niger River, and the Roman Catholics came in 1885.[11] By the mid-twentieth century most Igbo had adopted Christianity, though the tensile strength of Igbo traditional religion sustained millions of devotees as they developed a strong sense of ethnic identity. Igbo traditional religion requires the maintenance of a harmonious relationship with humanity and supernatural forces such as God, divinities, and ancestors.[12] This Igbo spirituality is often expressed through prayer, songs, arts, dance, myths, and so on, which Igbos have beautifully incorporated into Catholicism.

Although miles away from their homeland and having been

---

socio Demographic Profile in Comparison to Native Blacks," *Journal of Asian and African Studies*, 34 no. 2(1999):210-215. Kalu Ogbaa, *The Nigerian Americans* (Westport: Greenwood Press, 2003). R. Reynolds, "Bless this Little Time We Stayed Here: Prayers of Invocation As Mediation of Immigrant Experience Among Nigerians in Chicago," in *Ethnolinguistic Chicago: Language and Literacy in the City's Neighborhoods*, ed. M. Farr (New Jersey: Lawrence Erlbaum Associates, 2004), 161-187. J. Takuogang, "Contemporary African Immigrants to The Unites States." *A Journal of African Migration*, no.2 (September 2002), http://www.africamigration.com/issue_02.html [accessed August 9, 2013]. Ezekiel Umoh Ette, *Nigerian Immigrants in the United States: Race, Identity, and Acculturation* (New York: Lexington Books, 2012), 9-30.

[9] Onwughalu, 25.

[10] Reynolds, 183.

[11] Ikenga Ozigbo, *Roman Catholicism in Southern Nigeria 1985-1931*(Nigeria: Etukokwu Publishers Ltd, 1988),36-92.

[12] Alozie Onwubiko, *African Thought, Religion, and Culture* (Enugu: Snaap Press Ltd, 1991),59-63.

exposed for a long time to a different social and cultural life, many Igbo still have a strong nostalgia for their cultural heritage and are committed to preserving it. They often appreciate the need to educate their children in the culture of their progenitors through various means such as, festivals, traditional ceremonies, religious observances, and casual gatherings of fellow kinfolk. These nostalgic activities not only remind the Igbo of the land from which they emigrated, but also ensure the survival of their traditional values. Thus they are able to maintain and protect these values, norms, customs, and cultural identity on alien soil, and ensure their continued existence by passing them on to their American-born children.[13] In essence, Igbo communities were formed, first and foremost, to foster the preservation of the Igbo culture and tradition.

Igbo Catholics in the United States, though registered with parishes where they attend Mass in English, gather periodically at a certain parish church designated by the diocese to celebrate Mass as well as perform other liturgical activities in the Igbo language. In some of the designated parishes the Igbo Mass is celebrated every Sunday,[14] whereas it is celebrated once a month in others.[15]

B. Formation of Igbo Catholic Communities in America

Many immigrant ethnic groups in the United States, including the Igbo, have generally found it spiritually enriching to establish native church communities where they can experience liturgical worship in ways that are consistent with and meaningful to their native experience of church.[16] Such

---

[13] D.I Ndubuike, *The Struggles, Challenges, and Triumph of the African Immigrants in America* (New York: The Edwin Mellen Press, 2002), 108.

[14] Blessed Sacrament St. Charles Borromeo Roman Catholic Church, http://www.bsscb.org/index.cfm [accessed August 9, 2012].

[15] See, Nigerian Igbo Catholic Community Archdiocese of Baltimore, Maryland USA, http://niccchurch.org/index.html [accessed August 9, 2012], Igbo Catholic Community Archdiocese of Chicago and Environs, INNAC, http://igbocatholicschicago.org/ [accessed August 9, 2012], Igbo Catholic Community- Houston, ICCH, http://igbocatholicshouston.org/ [accessed August 9, 2012].

[16] According to the United States Conference of Catholics Bishops Office for the Pastoral Care of Migrants, Refugees and Travelers (PCMRT),

immigrant church communities are known to serve as avenues for community building, experiencing togetherness, overcoming cultural isolation, and providing a stronghold for advocacy programs that help children of immigrants and their families. Some Igbo immigrants in the United States yearn for a Eucharistic liturgy that expresses their traditional heritage conforming with how liturgical celebrations are performed in Nigerian Igbo churches. These yearnings began the quest for a need to have liturgical celebrations in the Igbo language and style in the United States for Igbos.

Liturgical celebrations such as weddings, child dedication, and funeral Masses, in the Igbo language date back to 1980 in the United States.[17] However, the celebration of the Catholic Mass in the Igbo language on a formal basis did not begin until 1994 in Houston, Texas.[18] The Igbo Catholic Community began remotely as distinct chapters in various U.S. cities before the chapters were amalgamated in 2003 at the Tenth Anniversary celebration of the Igbo Catholic Community in the Los Angeles Archdiocese, officiated by His Eminence Francis Cardinal Arinze, then Prefect of the Vatican's Congregation for Divine Worship and Discipline of the Sacraments.[19] It was at this special

---

there are 17 African cultural/ ethnic communities in the US: Burundi, Cameroon, Congo, Cape Verde, Eritrean and Ethiopian (Ge'ez rite), Ghanaian, Ivory Coast, Kenyan, Liberia, Nigerian, Rwandan, Sudanese, Tanzanian, Ugandan, Zairean, Zambian; 9 Caribbean Communities: Belize, Dominican Republic, Grenadian, Guyana, Haitian, Jamaican, Santa Lucian, Trinidad and Tobago; and 12 European Communities: Croatian, Czech, French, Irish, Italian, Lithuanian, Polish, Portuguese, Hungarian, Slovak, Slovenian, Ukrainian. Cf.
http://www.usccb.org/issues-and-action/cultural-diversity/pastoral-care-of-migrants-refugees-and-travelers/ethnic-ministries/, accessed [December 19, 2013], and http://www.usccb.org/issues-and-action/cultural-diversity/pastoral-care-of-migrants-refugees-and-travelers/ethnic-ministries/upload/ACC.pdf, accessed [December19, 2013].

[17] A detailed information on the formation of the Igbo catholic community can be found in; Igbo Catholic Community- Houston, ICCH, http://www.igbocatholicshouston.org/history.htm [accessed August 9, 2012].

[18] Ibid.

[19] According to the history on the formation of Igbo catholic community in the US, during the celebratory occasion, there was evidence of

occasion that the individual groups became consolidated to become "Igbo Catholic *Communities* USA."[20] However, in Baltimore, at the 2008 national convention of the nascent organization, the name for the organization was changed to "Igbo Catholic *Community* USA" (ICCUSA) to emphasize unity.[21] Today ICCUSA strives to maintain a permanent link between the Igbo immigrants and their native land through Igbo preservation of the Igbo culture and tradition in the Eucharistic liturgy and fostering the wellbeing of its members.

C. Incorporation of Igbo Culture and Traditions in the Eucharistic Liturgy

The Igbo generally worship in a style that reinforces their cultural identity[22] as is consistent with *Sacrosanctum Concilium*. The Igbo Catholic community makes room for liturgical and cultural diversity during its liturgical activities. Thus the Eucharistic liturgy is celebrated by means of a unique Igbo articulation and understanding of worship. Using the traditional language in worship, the community preserves Igbo culture and language both in the Eucharistic liturgy and other non-liturgical services, such as teaching the Igbo language, catechism classes, and Igbo religious hymns and songs to their children. The Igbo Mass celebrated in the United States, just as it is performed in Nigeria, features Igbo ethnic liturgical hymns, songs and music

---

delegates from other chapters who were present. Among the represented chapters were Igbo Catholic Community, Baltimore, MD; Igbo Catholic Community, Houston, TX; Igbo Catholic Community, Queens, NY; Nigerian Igbo Catholic Community, San Bernardino, CA; Nigeria Catholic Community, Washington, D.C.

[20] Igbo Catholic Community- Houston, ICCH, http://www.igbocatholicshouston.org/history.htm [accessed August 9, 2012].

[21] During this convention, an evolved understanding prevailed – one that saw association not as a gathering of separate Igbo Catholic communities, but as a nucleic realization of the one Igbo Catholic community with its branches spread across the United States.

[22] April Gordon, *Nigerian Diverse Peoples* (California: ABC-CLIO, Inc., 2003), 238.

with exotic musical instruments as well as the congregation wearing Igbo traditional attires.[23]

Structurally, the Igbo Mass, from the entrance to the dismissal rite, is celebrated the way most parishes celebrate in the U.S., but with unique Igbo flourishes. These adaptations in the Igbo Mass could be seen in the language, style of preaching, music and dance incorporated into the Mass, and in the manner in which the people celebrate the offertory.

Language of the Igbo Mass

Among the major achievements of *Sacrosactum Concilium* are articles[24] which encourage the use of the vernacular in the liturgy and the adaptation of the Roman rite to various cultures. These articles represent the Council's concrete response to the pastoral needs of the local churches. Language is the vessel that contains a people's culture, for, "Language is not only a mode of expressing the culture of its native speakers, but also is itself a part of that culture."[25] Language plays a vital role in religious worship, since it enhances an active participation of all involved in the ritual act. The main unifying cultural feature of the Igbo is their language, also called Igbo, which has many dialects. [26]

---

[23] Youtube Video: *Uka Nkuputanwa Iberosi Twins: Nigeria- Igbo Catholic Association Atlanta GA Mass in Igbo Language* [accessed April 7, 2013]; Youtube Video: *Igbo Catholic Community Harvest of 2007*, Newark NJ [accessed April 7, 2013].

[24] SC, 36-40.

[25] Igwe Osita Agwuna III, *Igbo People: A Language and A People* (Onitsha: Pioneer Printing Press, 1980), 29.

[26] Since there are seventeen different dialects of Igbo which often are not mutually intelligible to other Igbo speakers, a standard Igbo phonology called *"Igbo izugbe"* has been developed in the later part of the 20th century. This serves as the official accepted form of the language. Besides the various speech sounds peculiar to specific dialects, there are 36 letters of the Igbo alphabet, eight vowels sounds, and five "officially accepted" parts of speech in the Igbo language. Cf. Raphael Egwu, *Igbo Idea of the Supreme Being and the Triune God* (Germany: Echter Verlag Wurzburg, 1998), 30-34; Noam Chomsky and Morris Halle, *The Sound Pattern of English* (New York: Harper and Row, 1968); John A. Goldsmith, *AutoSegmental Phonology* (New York: Garland Publishers, 1979).

The Igbo Mass employs the Igbo language for the entire liturgy whether in Nigeria or in the United States. For the language of a people opens to them the spirit of the Church's liturgy, expressed in maximum, active, conscious, plenary and socio-communitarian participation in liturgical celebrations. [27] Thus, a full, conscious and active participation in liturgical celebrations is possible only if the worshipping community understands both the text and the ritual of the celebration.[28]

Igbo liturgical texts were produced in the 1900s, but more radical liturgical innovations began seriously in Nigerian Igbo Catholic churches in the 1970s with the translation and printing of the English-Latin Missal to Igbo language called *Usoro Emume Nke Missa*.[29] The Igbo missal, which had the Sunday reading and prayers of all the three cycles of the Roman Missal was translated by several people on their own and was used by different parishes in Nigeria beginning in 1974.[30] In 1977, a number of other liturgical and catechetical books, such as the text for the celebration of the sacraments, *Usoro Emume Sacrament, Katekisim Igbo* (Igbo Catechism*), and Katekisma Nk'Okwukwe Nzuko Katolik N'Asusu Igbo* (Catechism of the Catholic Faith in Igbo Language), were translated and produced for an active participation of Igbo Catholics in the liturgy.[31] By

---

[27] Patrick Chibuko, Patrick Chibuko, "Dialectics of Language in the liturgy" (Lecture, Catholic Institute of West Africa, Port Harcourt Nigeria, April 28, 2008).

[28] Cf. SC,36.

[29] The Episcopal Conference of Nigeria and the Sacred Congregation of Divine Worship. *Usoro Emume Nke Missa (*Ibadan: The Catholic Bishops of East Central State, Nigeria: 1973).it is important to note that this liturgical text contains only the preface and Eucharistic prayers in Igbo , English, and Latin.

[30] Ikenga Ozigbo, *Igbo Catholicism: The Onitsha Connection 1967-1984* (Ibadan: Africana-Fep Publishers Limited, 1985), 33.

[31] It is important to note here that the first translation of the Catechism in Igbo language was done by Fr. Aime Ganot, and C.Vogler and L.Lejeune (Spiritans who were on mission in Nigeria) produced the Catechism of the Catholic Faith in the Igbo Language; A Gnot, *Katekismi Ibo*, Roman Catholic Mission, Onitsha Lower Niger (Paris:1901); C.Vogler and L.Lejeune, *Katekisma Nk'Okwukwe Nzuko Katolik N'Asusu Igbo,* Roman Catholic Mission, Onitsha Southern Nigeria(Strasbourg:1903).Further reading on the translation of liturgical texts into Igbo language could be found in Donatus E.O Ogudo, *The*

1983, a translation of the Sunday readings and prayers for every Sunday, Solemnity, and Holy Week, was produced by the Igbo-Speaking Bishops of Nigeria, and entitled, *Akwukwo Misa – The Missal*. This translation called *Akwukwo Misa*, is been used to celebrate the Igbo Mass both in Nigeria and in the United States.

Music and Dance in the Igbo Mass

For Igbos, the liturgy is a joyful celebration. Songs give sweetness to the expression of prayer; promote the union of minds, and make rites more solemn, by rooting them in a person's culture. [32] Singing is an essential part of the solemn liturgy of the Church, and every liturgical celebration liturgy should always be marked by the presence of songs as the church rightly expresses in *Sacrosanctum Concilium*, "The musical tradition of the universal Church is a treasure of inestimable value, greater even than that of any other art. The main reason for this pre-eminence is that, as sacred song united to the words, it forms a necessary or integral part of the solemn liturgy." [33] Herein lies the motivation for the composition of Igbo songs whose text and music will be worthy of the worship of God.

Virtually all Nigerian cultures have their own traditions of music and dance, which are central to the way Nigerians remember their past and celebrate their present.[34] In fact music and dance are often central to specific events such as: worship, title taking, naming ceremonies, town festivals, harvest, victory

---

Catholic Missionaries and the Liturgical Movement in Nigeria: An Historical Overview, (Paderborn:Verlag Bonifatius-Druckerei,1988), 64-72. Donatus Ogudo has a detailed topic on Liturgico-Catechetical Texts in the Vernacular.

[32] Patrick Chibuko, "Dialectics of Language in the liturgy" (Lecture, Catholic Institute of West Africa, Port Harcourt Nigeria, April 28, 2008).

[33] SC, 112.

[34] For further reading on music as a representation of cultural style, see Jeff Todd Titon, *Worlds of Music: An Introduction to the Music of the World's Peoples* (London: Collier Macmillan, 1984).

at war, initiation rites, etc.[35] As with most Christianized people, the Igbo people incorporate many of their indigenous cultural values, customs, and traditions into their Christian worship. In the Igbo Mass, religious dances are sometimes performed at different moments during the liturgy: entrance procession, Gospel procession,[36] during offertory, and at the recessional.[37] *Sacrosanctum Concilium* asserts:

> In certain countries, especially in mission lands there are people who have their own musical tradition and this plays a great part in their religious and social life. For this reason their music should be held in proper esteem and a suitable place is to be given to it, not only in forming their religious sense but also in adapting worship to their native genius.[38]

The tunes and local musical accompaniment bring to light the culture of the people which has been incorporated into their Christian worship, gearing towards an active, conscious participation in the Eucharistic Liturgy. Songs and dances are accompanied with traditional instruments such as, drums of different sizes and intensity, wooden gongs of various dimensions, flutes of diverse size and tone, stringed instruments, xylophones, earthenware pots, and metal gongs.[39]

---

[35] For an example of traditional Igbo dance see, Special Igbo Cultural Dance, http://www.youtube.com/watch?v=CmOKYR-C4dg&feature=relmfu[accessed August 9, 2013].

[36] During the gospel procession, a "town crier" often announces the arrival of the book of the gospel and invites all to be attentive and to listen to the "Word of God," which is our source of spiritual nourishment. This procession is accompanied by appropriate hymns and dancers who usher in the Gospel.

[37] In most Catholic parishes in Nigeria, this religious dance is common in most liturgical celebrations like Christmas, Christ the King, Easter, Ordination of priests, religious professions, etc, and has been adopted by Igbo immigrants in the United States.

[38] *SC, 119.*

[39] Example of these instruments include inter alia;1) *Ekwe (Slit drum):* This wooden musical instrument is a very powerful and effective means of communication. The instrument also comes in a smaller size known as the *okpokolo.*;2) *Ogene (Metal gong):* The *ogene* is a hollow metal gong about one foot long and oval, often with a handle at one end, and it is

The kind of liturgical music and dance used in the Igbo Mass is one that is not foreign but part and parcel of the people's way of life. It should be clear that the dance is not there for recreation or entertainment, but for prayer, which is the raising of minds and hearts to God through bodily gestures and movements, for "when the Church prays or sings or acts, the faith of those taking part is nourished and their minds are

---

played by hitting methodically with a piece of hardwood;3) *Udu (Clay pot):Udu* is percussion instrument made form pottery. Some of these pots, especially the small clay pots used for dancing, have a perforation on the upper side of the body. It is played with the palms of the hand or soft pads, but the left and right hands control the holes at the side and top of the *udu* respectively; 4) *Ichaka* (Rattle):This musical instrument is fashioned from the calabash, a tropical African plant of the bignonia family, bearing large, gourdlike fruit. The instrument is made by stringing hundreds of tiny beads all around the dried calabash fruit. The beads strung around it produce a rattling sound when the instrument is shaken; 5) *Oja* (Flute): The *oja* is the most common of the woodwind instruments. A melodious instrument, it is able to produce the first five notes of the diatonic scale. Structurally, it has three holes two at the sides and one at the bottom. A curved opening is made at the top where the lips rest as air is blown into the flute; 6) *Igba* (Drum): *Igba* is the chief among the percussion instruments constructed from soft wood cylinders with open ended bottoms and a top sealed with dry animal skin leather; 7) *Ngedegwu/ Ngelenge* (Xylophone): *Ngedegwu* is regarded as a melodic instrument made of strands from a special wood and sounds like the western piano. For further reading on Igbo musical instruments see; N.S Onuigbo, *The Three Worlds in Igbo Traditional Religion* (Enugu: Delta Publication, 2009), 141-188. Patrick Chibuko, *Paschal Mystery of Christ Foundation for Liturgical Inculturation in Africa* (Enugu: Snaap Press Ltd, 2001),157-158. Joy Nwosu, "Classification of Igbo Musical Instruments," *Nigerian Magazine* 144(1983):38-58. Azubike Ifionu, "Igbo Music and Dance," *Groundwork on Igbo History* (1992):720-742. *N Okaosa*," Ibo Musical Instruments," *Nigerian Magazine* 75 (December1962):4-14. Traditional Musical instruments: Igbo Ogene Anuka Gong (bell) http://www.the-nigeria.com/2011/11/traditional-musical-instruments-igbo.html#!/2011/11/traditional-musical-instruments-igbo.html[accessed August 9, 2013]. Samples of Musical Instruments from the Igboland, http://www.umunna.org/instruments.html [accessed December 27, 2012]. Igbo Culture, Traditions and History, http://enyi-oha-one-of-naiji.blogspot.com/2012/02/traditional-igbo-music-drums-and-flutes.html [accessed August 9, 2013].

raised to God, so that they may offer Him their rational service and more abundantly receive His grace."[40]

Preaching

Preaching in an Igbo Mass is performed by the priest using various forms and styles. Many Igbo priests begin their sermon with a popular hymn or chorus to dispose the congregation to be active listeners, so they can receive the message. Thus we see music playing yet another role in the Mass during the Liturgy of the Word. Effective preachers choose appropriate hymns or choruses that reflect the theme of the homily and readings for the day, or they might begin with a series of interpellations to which the congregation responds with effective gusto. A common pattern of the interpellation is as follows:

> Priest: Otito diri Jesu (Praise be to Jesus)
> People: Na ndu ebebe (Forever and ever)
> Priest: Onye jisie ike (Whoever is steadfast in faith)
> People: O ruo ana eze (makes heaven)
> Priest: Onye jekata ghalu (If one should backslide in faith)
> People: Nwanne ya enyelu ya aka (Let him or her be supported in faith by the brethren)[41]

Some priests employ the dialogue method, which involves asking relevant questions related to the readings of the day or asking a member of the congregation to share his or her reflection on the readings. Others choose the storytelling method, possibly using stories from traditional folklore to drive home a point or deliver the inspired message. There are yet others who preach by delivering their homily straightforwardly, using only gestures and relevant movements. Therefore, these methods of preaching the Word of God in the original language of the people with such dynamism elicit both devotion and active participation in the liturgy.

---

[40] SC,33.

[41] This interpellation is commonly used by Igbo priests both in Nigeria and has found its way into the sermons of Igbo Masses celebrated in the US.

Offertory

The offertory procession, according to the Roman rite, involves the singing of the offertory hymn and a procession to the altar with the bread and wine to be offered, which are then presented to the priest by those selected to bring forth the gifts. Also money and other gifts for the poor and the church may be collected or brought forward at this time.[42] In the Igbo Mass, however, offertory involves a procession of the entire assembly accompanied with singing, dancing, and clapping, as they present their gifts at the altar of the Lord.[43] The offertory hymns are carefully chosen to inspire active participation and generous donations of cash offerings at the collection boxes/baskets which are normally placed before the sanctuary, or at other strategic locations in the church.[44] Non-monetary gifts are also common and welcome. Even when people have nothing to offer, they are encouraged to stand up and go to the collection boxes/baskets empty-handed as a sign of self-offering to God. [45] The offertory music is very animated, exciting, and inspiring, and usually lasts a relatively long time, given that the whole assembly has to dance with exuberance to the altar, to present their offerings. Even though this method of offertory is time consuming, no one seems to be in a hurry.

Compared to the placing of gifts in a basket passed around during time for offertory, known as the secret-bag method of collection introduced by the missionaries, the Igbo style of offering of gifts is seen as yielding more active participation in the liturgy.[46] The secret-bag collection, as it were, did not allow

---

[42] *Institutio Generalis Missalis Romani(General Instruction on the Roman Missal)*An English Language Study Translation by the Secretariat for the Liturgy of the National Conference of Catholic Bishops(U.S.A: 2000), nr.73.

[43] Elochukwu Uzukwu, *Worship as Body Language* (Minnesota: The Liturgical Press, 1997), 273.

[44] Youtube Video: Uka Nkuputanwa Iberosi Twins: Nigeria- Igbo Catholic Association Atlanta GA Mass in Igbo Language [accessed August 9, 2013].

[45] Patrick Chibuko, "Alternative Order of Eucharistic Celebration: A Case for Local Churches in Nigeria," *Journal of Inculturation Theology 10*, no. 1(April 2008):54.

[46] Elochukwu Uzukwu, 273.

people the opportunity to personally present their offering to God in a more direct and visible fashion, as one would before a deity in the Igbo traditional religion, for instance. The present method of singing and dancing to the sanctuary to present gifts, is a striking adaptation of Igbo custom to the Eucharistic liturgy.[47] It also demonstrates the genius of the people, and makes them active participants in the liturgical celebration.

D. Significance of the Igbo Mass for Immigrants

The Nigerian Igbo Catholic Community in the United States serves as an avenue for community building, experiencing togetherness, overcoming cultural isolation, and providing a stronghold for advocacy programs that help children of immigrants and their families. The Igbo Mass has further helped Nigerian Igbo immigrants increase their self-esteem as they sustain and foster their ethnic identity in a foreign land.[48] This self-awareness invariably fosters self-identity and builds personal strengths such as courage, persistence, creativity, stronger interpersonal relationships in an immigrant community. More concretely, this opportunity to worship in a familiar language and style provides an environment for all Igbos to worship in their native language. It also helps Igbo immigrants to promote their religious and cultural heritage as a people, maintain the Igbo Catholic identity and tradition which is under threat of assimilation in the United States, provide spiritual guidance to Igbo children, and promote cultural awareness among the younger generation of the Igbo community.[49] Although this faith community has become an avenue where young Igbo-Americans learn the Igbo language, most of the younger generation are not able to speak the language fluently.[50] The various Igbo Catholic community chapters need

---

[47] Ibid.,273; Patrick Chibuko, "Alternative Order of Eucharistic Celebration: A Case for Local Churches in Nigeria,"151 71.

[48] Moses Biney, *Singing the Lord's Song in a Foreign Land in African Immigrant Religions in America*, ed. Olupona, Jacob and Regina Gemignani (New York: New York university press, 2007), 276.

[49] Frank Okechukwu, interview by author, South Bend, IN, April 3, 2012.

[50] This is my observation having visited many Igbo catholic families in Chicago and its environs, and attended other social gatherings organized by Igbo in the United States.

to find other avenues that will help the younger generation learn the language better within the Eucharistic liturgy. One way may be involving children more in the readings at an Igbo Mass, providing Mass bulletins that are written in Igbo language, and supporting their language acquisition at home.

Despite the aforementioned challenge, the Igbo Mass offers attainment of the fullness of being for the Igbo, as their identity becomes both an ingredient and product of communality. Beyond the question of identity formation and preservation of heritages, the communities also function as support networks, which benefit members in areas such job search, the securing of health and life insurance, and mortgages. [51]

Conclusion

The Igbo Mass fulfills the yearnings of many Nigerian Igbo immigrants who are unfamiliar with, or often feel lost in, or alienated from, the Western style of worship. Since ritual plays a powerful role in worship, namely drawing people into the realm of the sacred, there is a deeper appreciation of the Igbo mass because a larger sense of continuity is preserved in the liturgy; evident in the incorporation or integration of cultural praxis in the liturgy.[52] Additionally, this faith community aims at sharing the Igbo culture with the whole of the parishes where it exists, parishes which, in turn, serve as the medium of contact and locus for the development of a working relationship between Igbo Catholic immigrants and the United States Conference of Catholic Bishops, on the one hand, and with other ethnic communities, on the other. Through these faith communities Igbos contribute to the fostering of the Catholic faith in a most unique and positive way.

---

[51] Austin Okigbo, interview by author, South Bend, IN, April 9, 2012. Fr. Austin Okigbo is an Igbo Catholic priest and an assistant professor of ethnomusicology at the University of Colorado Boulder. He holds a Ph.D. in ethnomusicology and African Studies. Fr. Okigbo pioneered the beginning of the Igbo catholic community of the Delaware valley in 2000.

[52] Donatus Chukwu, interview by author, South Bend, IN, March 13, 2012.

Furthermore, the Igbo Catholic community, to a great extent, is engaged in forging new identities by utilizing several cultural tools and activities, including language education and the observation of festivals obtainable in their home countries. Also, it creates the forum for individuals to build social capital and support networks, to assist them in addressing some of the general challenges they face as immigrants such as adapting to their new environment, employment, social and cultural shocks, supporting family members back in Nigeria, identity issues, housing, and racism.[53]

Finally, from this study, it is evident that liturgy is not only the place where we lift up our hearts in worship to God, it is also a place where ethnic identities can be formed and cultural values preserved to posterity.

---

[53] For further reading on the Challenges of Igbo immigrants in the US, See Obiefuna Onwughalu, *Parents' Involvement in Education: The Experience of an African Immigrant Community in Chicago* (Bloomington:iUniverse, Inc.:2011), 30-33 and Ezekiel Umoh Ette, *Nigerian Immigrants in the United States: Race, Identity, and Acculturation* (New York: Lexington Books, 2012), 122-139.

1. Pictures

MAP OF IGBOLAND [54]

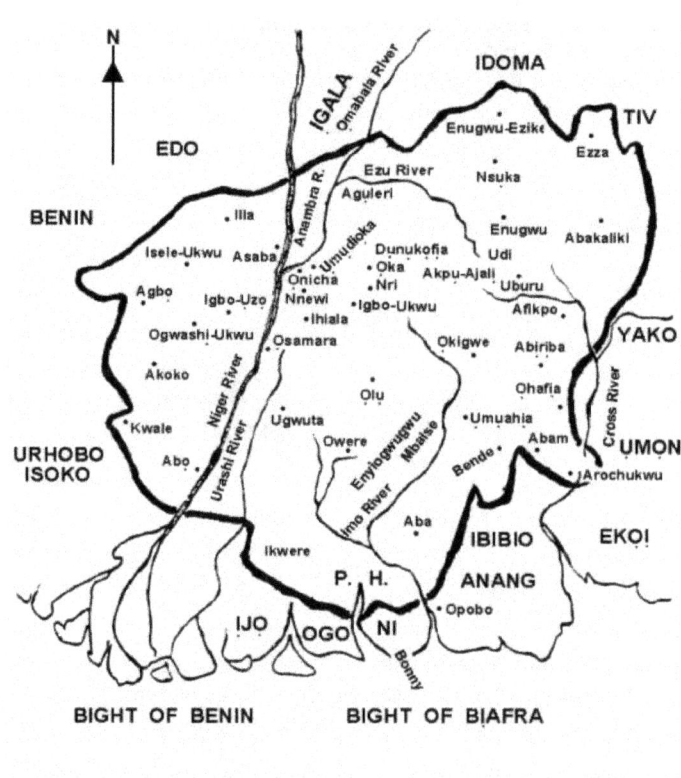

---

[54] Map extracted from Nigerian Wiki.
http://nigerianwiki.com/wiki/Igbo_people [accessed August 9, 2013].

Works Cited

Agwuna, Igwe Osita. *Igbo People: A Language and A People.* Onitsha: Pioneer Printing Press, 1980.

Biney, Moses. *Singing the Lord's Song in a Foreign Land in African Immigrant Religions in America.* Edited by Olupona, Jacob and Regina Gemignani. New York: New York University Press, 2007.

Blessed Sacrament St. Charles Borromeo Roman Catholic Church, http://www.bsscb.org/index.cfm[accessed September 8, 2012].

Chibuko, Patrick. *Paschal Mystery of Christ Foundation for Liturgical Inculturation in Africa.* Enugu: Snaap Press Ltd, 2001.

-----. "Alternative Order of Eucharistic Celebration: A Case for Local Churches in Nigeria," *Journal of Inculturation Theology* 10, no.1 (April 2008):51-71.

-----. "Dialectics of Language in the Liturgy" 5

Chomsky, Noam and Morris Halle. *The Sound Pattern of English.* New York: Harper and Row, 1968.

Djamba,Y.K. "African Immigrants in the United States: A socio Demographic Profile in Comparison to Native Blacks." *Journal of Asian and African Studies*, 34 no 2(1999):210-215,

Ebaugh, Helen and Janet Chafetz. *Religion and the New Immigrants.* California: Alta Mira Press, 2000.

Egwu, Raphael. *Igbo Idea of the Supreme Being and the Triune God.* Germany: Echter Verlag Wurzburg, 1998.

Ejizu, Christopher. "The Traditional Igbo Perception of Reality: Its Dialectics and Dilemma," *Bigard Theological Studies* 9 (1989):58-73.

Eluwa, G. et al. *A History of Nigeria for Schools and College.* Nigeria: Africana- FEP Publishers, 1988.

Ette, Umoh Ezekiel. *Nigerian Immigrants in the United States: Race, Identity, and Acculturation*. New York: Lexington Books, 2012.

Goldsmith, John A. *AutoSegmental Phonology* . New York: Garland Publishers, 1979.

Gordon April. *Nigerian Diverse Peoples*. California: ABC-CLIO, Inc., 2003.

Ifionu, Azubike. "Igbo Music and Dance," *Groundwork on Igbo History* (1992):720-742.

Igbo Catholic Community Archdiocese of Chicago and Environs, INNAC, http://igbocatholicschicago.org/ [accessed August 9, 2013].

Igbo Catholic Community- Houston, ICCH, http://igbocatholicshouston.org/ [accessed August 9, 2013].

Igbo Catholic Community Church Newark NJ, http://www.youtube.com/user/iccnewark/featured [accessed August 9, 2013].

Igbo Culture Traditions and History, http://enyi-oha-one-of-naiji.blogspot.com/2012/02/traditional-igbo-music-drums-and-flutes.html [accessed August 9, 2013].

Igbo Mass for The Dedication and Baptism of the Iberosi twin girls on September 11, 2011," http://www.youtube.com/watch?v=g2RqHZ9YzN0 [accessed August 9, 2013].

Institutio Generalis Missalis Romani (*General Instruction on the Roman Missal*) An English Language Study Translation by the Secretariat for the Liturgy of the National Conference of Catholic Bishops (U.S.A: 2000).

McNally, Melissa. African Catholics Build Community in Archdiocese; Igbo Masses Help Connect U.S., Nigerian Experience, posted online 08/09/06, http://www.rcan.org/index.cfm?fuseaction=feature.show&feature_id=262 [accessed August 9, 2013].

Ndubuike, D.I. *The Struggles, Challenges, and Triumph of the African Immigrants in America*. New York: The Edwin Mellen Press, 2002.

Nigeria High Commission London,
August 9, 2013].

Nigerian Igbo Catholic Community Archdiocese of Baltimore, Maryland USA, http://niccchurch.org/index.html [accessed September 8, 2012].

Nigerian Wiki. http://nigerianwiki.com/wiki/Igbo_people [accessed August 9, 2013].

Nigeria Single Bells, http://overseasconnection.com/public_html/bells/nigerian_single_bells.html [accessed August 9, 2013].

Nwosu, Joy."Classification of Igbo Musical Instruments," *Nigerian Magazine 144(1983):38-58*.

Ogbaa, Kalu. *The Nigerian Americans*. Westport: Greenwood Press, 2003.

Ogudo, Donatus. *The Catholic Missionaries and the Liturgical Movement in Nigeria: An Historical Overview*. Paderborn:Verlag Bonifatius-Druckerei,1988.

Okaosa, N. "Ibo Musical Instruments," *Nigerian Magazine 75. (December1962):4-14*.

Onwubiko, Alozie. *African Thought, Religion, and Culture*. Enugu: Snaap Press Ltd, 1991.

Onwughalu, Obiefuna. *Parents' Involvement in Education: The Experience of an African Immigrant Community in Chicago*. Bloomington: iUniverse, Inc.:2011.

Onuigbo,N.S. *The Three Worlds in Igbo Traditional Religion*. Enugu: Delta Publication, 2009.

Ozigbo, Ikenga. *Igbo Catholicism: The Onitsha Connection 1967-1984*. Ibadan: Africana-Fep Publishers Limited, 1985.

PortCities Bristol, Copyright BCC Museum 2003, http://discoveringbristol.org.uk/browse/slavery/category/sl ave-trade/P2830/[accessed August 9, 2013].

Reynolds, R . "Bless this Little Time We Stayed Here: Prayers of Invocation As Mediation of Immigrant Experience Among Nigerians in Chicago" in *Ethnolinguistic Chicago: Language and Literacy in the City's Neighborhoods.* Edited by Farr M. New Jersey: Lawrence Erlbaum Associates, 2004.

Samples of Musical Instruments from the Igboland, http://www.umunna.org/instruments.html [accessed August 9, 2013].

Second Vatican Council. *Sacrosanctum Concilium* [Constitution on the Sacred Liturgy]. December 4, 1963. In *The Sixteen Documents of Vatican II,* 47-83. Edited by Marianne L Trouve. Boston: Pauline Books, 1999.

Special Igbo Cultural Dance, http://www.youtube.com/watch?v=CmOKYR-C4dg&feature=relmfu [accessed August 9, 2013].

Takuogang, J. *Contemporary African Immigrants to the United States.* Irinkkerindo: *A Journal of African Migration,* http://www.africamigration.com/archive_02/j_takougang.h tm [accessed August 9, 2013].

The Episcopal Conference of Nigeria and the Sacred Congregation of Divine Worship. *Usoro Emume Nke Missa.* Ibadan: The Catholic Bishops of East Central State, Nigeria: 1973.

The Sacred Arts & Sciences of the Igbo People, http://igbocybershrine.com/category/mythology/ [accessed August 9, 2013].

Titon, Jeff Todd. *Worlds of Music: An Introduction to the Music of the World's Peoples.* London: Collier Macmillan, 1984.

Traditional Musical instruments: Igbo Ogene Anuka Gong (bell) http://www.the-nigeria.com/2011/11/traditional-musical-instruments-igbo.html#!/2011/11/traditional-musical-instruments-igbo.html [accessed August 9, 2013].

United States Conference of Catholics Bishops Office for the Pastoral Care of Migrants, Refugees and Travelers (PCMRT), http://www.usccb.org/issues-and-action/cultural-diversity/pastoral-care-of-migrants-refugees-and-travelers/ethnic-ministries/, [accessed December 19, 2013].

Uzukwu, Elochukwu. *Worship as Body Language.* Minnesota: The Liturgical Press, 1997.

-----. *Inculturation a Nigerian perspective.* Enugu: Spiritan Press, 1988.

Williams, Lizzie. *Nigeria: The Bradt Travel Guide.* UK: Bradt Travel Guides, 2008.

Building a Story Together:
The Challenge of Conversion in a Plural Age:
A Narrative Interpretation

Nathaniel Samuel, Ph.D.
St. Thomas University
Miami Gardens, Florida

Abstract

If Christian conversion is understood as conversion-in-history, then how does our present culture of fear, distrust and indifference to the 'other' animate discipleship as an ongoing process of conversion? This essay develops a narrative hermeneutic as a viable conceptual and theological framework for engaging this question. Describing the conversion process as an unfolding story of our lived "yes" to God's self-gift, it argues that saying "yes" to God today means, among other things, welcoming the (often demanding) story of the other. The "yes" of conversion entails nurturing a narrative hospitality. The essay offers two ways to practice a spatially and temporally responsible narrative hospitality that are urgent for Christian discipleship today.

Keywords: Conversion; narrative; pluralism; narrative hermeneutics; hospitality; identity; empathy.

The Story of Now[1]: Fear, Indifference and Violence in the Encounter with the 'Other'

One year after the tragic events at the finish line of the 2013 Boston Marathon, I continue to be struck by a particular rhetoric, embraced by various media and public officials, claiming that the events of last April 15th have not and will not change who we are. Now, this statement may be interpreted in a number of ways. On the one hand, the tragedy revealed the best of who we are as a nation. The people of Boston triumphed as a community of resilience and compassion. Addressing an interfaith service of healing at Trinity Chapel, Copley Square in the aftermath of the tragedy, the Reverend Liz Walker (of

---

[1] Marshall Ganz, "Why Stories Matter: The Art and Craft of Social Change," *Sojourners Magazine* 38, no. 3 (2009).

Roxbury Presbyterian Church) captured well the texture of a heroic and compassionate community:

> This is what I know: God is here, in the midst of this sacred gathering, in this sanctuary and beyond. Different faiths, different races, strangers bound first by loss and pain, but now clinging together in growing strength, in a city that has always faced the darkness head on. We are members of one another; a community of resilience; hard pressed but not defeated; confounded, but not consumed. We are gathered in community, and through the blur of each other's tears, and the beats of so many broken hearts, we will rise in community and face whatever the future holds, resolutely as one. This is what is demanded of us, and this is who we are.[2]

Surely, we should remain steady in our compassion and resilience. However, it is quite another matter to say that the events of April 2013 should not *change* us – should not cause a critical reevaluation of the stories that we live by in this world, and how our national narratives may or may not fuel such instances of unadulterated rage and hate. Surely our continued development as a nation and global citizen demands such introspection at institutional and personal levels, leaving open a vision of change to ever-greater responsibility and to an authentic, inclusive humanism.

Changing who we are is the substance of a conversion narrative. It is an existential need that people of faith are called to discern in every age, as we further God's reign. The specific claim made by *this moment in history* on the Christian vocation to conversion is where I wish to focus this essay. Conversion is always *conversion-in-history*, so it bears asking: what specific claim does our moment in history impose on us?

I accentuate one particular claim in this essay. The events in Boston were, I suggest, emblematic of a more ubiquitous and persisting phenomenon: our fear, distrust and indifference to the presence of the 'other,' represented under the different

---

[2] "Interfaith Service for Bombing Victims in Boston." C-Span Video Library. Accessed May 22, 2013. http://www.c-spanvideo.org/program/BombingVi.

guises of the 'religious other', the 'racial other', the 'ethnic other', the 'poor and oppressed' other, and also the 'forgotten' other, meaning those who are othered by temporal distance and by memory.³ The problem may be summarized by an aporia adapted from German Lutheran scholar Eberhard Jüngel: "There *you* are – here *I* am! How does that concern me?"⁴ In other words, does the other make a claim on me, and is this claim legitimate? Does the present "clash of civilizations," heralded by scholars and social commentators, demand that we retreat into the bunkers of our familiar cultural values and norms – as Samuel Huntington would have us to do?⁵ Are we to engage the other, in our midst and in our memory, through exclusion or through the openness of embrace and hospitality?⁶

Thick Questions about Conversion

This trajectory in the story of now suggests a few thick questions about what constitutes a historically relevant conversion. How does this trajectory of otherness contextualize and make concrete the demands of discipleship as ongoing conversion in faith? Alternatively stated, how can we grow closer to God, as persons and as communities, as we engage the 'other' in our societies, in the knowledge that this 'other' may be

---

³As a society we are all too often indifferent to the global poor; we commonly distrust the Arab-featured passenger on our airline flight; we are all too quick to reduce the problem of violence in our inner cities to the dimensions of a 'Black' or Latino problem. Pluralism and difference permeates our social and cultural landscape and challenges our deepest sense of identity and morality.

⁴Eberhard Jüngel, "The Effectiveness of Christ Withdrawn: On the Process of Historical Understanding as an Introduction to Christology," in *Theological Essays I*, ed. J. B. Webster (Edinburgh, Scotland: T & T Clark, 1989).

⁵Samuel P. Huntington, *The Clash of Civilizations and the Remaking of World Order* (New York: Simon & Schuster, 2003), 21. See also Samuel P. Huntington, *Who Are We?: The Challenges to America's National Identity* (New York: Simon & Schuster Paperbacks, 2004).

⁶Miroslav Volf, *Exclusion and Embrace: A Theological Exploration of Identity, Otherness, and Reconciliation* (Nashville: Abingdon Press, 1996), 75. Volf describes exclusion as manifesting by way of elimination, assimilation, domination or abandonment. See also Amartya Sen, *Identity and Violence: The Illusion of Destiny* (New York: Norton, 2007) for similar critique of the clash of civilizations.

someone in need of our charity and justice, or may be a terrorist who may maim or kill? "There *you* are – here *I* am! How does that concern me?" Such questions are never easy, and this essay can hardly presume to offer definitive answers. But the challenge of making faith relevant in any age is to respond with wisdom, critical insight, and deep regard to its demands.

I offer a narrative hermeneutic as fecund for constructing an approach to these questions. Specifically, this essay makes three main points:

1. That a narrative hermeneutic is a viable conceptual framework, which characterizes the encounter with the other as a *narrative encounter*, and that the challenge therein regards a *re-storying* of identity.

2. That a narrative hermeneutic is also *theologically* viable for addressing this problem. I offer that a theological ethic of affirmation (or "yes," to God's self-gift) may be embodied in a practice of *narrative hospitality* – welcoming the storied lives of others, and sharing our lived stories.

3. That conversion, as the unfolding of our lived 'Yes' to God's self-gift, may be occasioned by the encounter with the other.

Hopefully, these proposals will constitute a response to the obvious question of: why a narrative approach to conversion?

The Conceptual Adequacy of a Narrative Hermeneutic

Regarding the conceptual adequacy of a narrative hermeneutic: "There *you* are – here *I* am! How does that concern me?" How can this question be viewed as 1) a *narrative encounter* that 2) invites a *re-storying of identity*? I suggest three main lines of questioning:

1. What is narrative?

2. How do narratives function?

3. What are the components of narrative identity? How does this clarify the term 're-storying'?

What is Narrative?

Narrative is quite a ubiquitous and pluriform phenomena, at least in popular usage. We are used to the standard definition of narrative as pertaining to the combination of events in literary plot. Yet, theorists in narrative psychology have long attested that human identity is ultimately an ongoing story (or at least a confluence of many stories), and that narrative is a form of cognitive competence that gives structure and meaning to day-to-day experience.[7] Even beyond personal narratives, there are also national narratives that constitute the ethos in which we exist as social beings. We are – as philosopher Paul Ricoeur was wont to say – beings "*entangled in stories.*"[8]

Such conceptual extensions of narrativity beyond discursive media have, however, failed to gain much traction in philosophical exploration. Under the sway of the linguistic turn in continental philosophy, narrative theorists (including Paul Ricoeur) have tended to concentrate on the functioning of literary text as the archetypal form of narrativity, perpetuating what Calvin Schrag has called an "excessive and self-limiting preoccupation with discourse and discursive practices" within contemporary philosophy.[9] On the evidence of current scholarship, therefore, it seems that there is much room for

---

[7]Jerome S. Bruner, *Actual Minds, Possible Worlds* (Cambridge, MA.: Harvard University Press, 1986); Jerome S. Bruner, "The Narrative Construction of "Reality"," in *Psychoanalysis and Development: Representations and Development*, ed. Massimo Ammaniti and Daniel N. Stern, Psychoanalytic Crosscurrents (New York: New York University Press, 1994); Stephen Crites, "Storytime: Recollecting the Past and Projecting the Future," in *Narrative Psychology: The Storied Nature of Human Conduct*, ed. Theodore R. Sarbin (New York: Praeger, 1986); Stephen Crites, "The Narrative Quality of Experience," in *Why Narrative?: Readings in Narrative Theology*, ed. Stanley Hauerwas and L. Gregory Jones (Grand Rapids, Mich.: W.B. Eerdmans, 1989); Donald Polkinghorne, *Narrative Knowing and the Human Sciences.*, ed. Lenore Langsdorf, Suny Series in Philosophy of the Social Sciences (Albany: State University of New York Press, 1988); Theodore R. Sarbin, ed. *Narrative Psychology: The Storied Nature of Human Conduct* (New York: Praeger, 1986).

[8]Paul Ricoeur, "Life in Quest of Narrative," in *On Paul Ricoeur: Narrative and Interpretation*, ed. David Wood (London: Routledge, 1991), 30.

[9]Calvin O. Schrag, *Communicative Praxis and the Space of Subjectivity* (Bloomington: Indiana University Press, 1986), 11.

establishing a more cohesive understanding of narrativity, if at all possible.

Narrative as a Human Competency to Establish a Storied World

But, this is a big 'if.' Theorizing on narrativity is made complex by the pluriformity and ubiquity of the phenomena. I propose, therefore, as a working definition, that narrative be understood as *a distinct human competency for forming meaningful connections among events, situations, causes, goals and other phenomena in life*. This narrative competency may congeal in many forms, including literary text. But, more significant to the purposes of this essay, it also extends to the actions and practices of daily life (non-discursive forms of expression) that are *lived narratives*, which express, constitute and embody our sense of identity and life story. The amalgam of such discursive and non-discursive forms of communication constitutes the storied world in which life unfolds as meaningful and livable. In essence, *narrative is a human competency to establish a storied, meaningful world*.

Narrative Encounters and the Mediation of Human Meaning

How do narratives function? A particularly evocative thesis of Paul Ricoeur is that narratives serve, among other things, to *mediate* the creation and transformation of meaning. Literary narratives (the textual archetype) enable a re-visioning of ordinary life by shepherding readers into the imagistic world of the text.[10] This narrative encounter with a text affords the critical distance necessary for 1) recognizing the ways in which we are socialized (often unconsciously) into our storied/symbolic cultural landscape, and 2) imaginatively reconfiguring of our agency in that world.[11]

---

[10] To be sure, Ricoeur was arguably under no illusion that literary text exhausted the potential for narrativity; rather, he focused on literature in its capacity as a *textual archetype*. It most perfectly possesses the compositional and textual qualities that make for good mediation. Ricoeur would further argue that storytelling gives authors ultimate flexibility to craft virtually an infinite number of plot variations (and thus worlds) that may engage the human imagination.

[11] Paul Ricoeur, *Time and Narrative*, trans., Kathleen Blamey and David Pellauer, 3 vols. (Chicago: The University of Chicago Press, 1984-1988).

I propose, however, that Ricoeur's thoughts must be extended to account for the ubiquity of narrative forms and narrative encounters observed earlier.[12] In particular, I offer that our lived narratives may also mediate human meaning. We are moved by life stories, not just biographies, but by our flesh and blood encounters, our personal relationships with charismatic individuals, saints and exemplars. Ricoeur has argued that human action is text and, as such, can mediate meaning.[13] I suggest that he does not preclude that action can do this in its capacity as lived narrative.

Dan McAdams and the Storied Nature of Personal (and National) Identity

It is now possible to clarify the term re-storying. Narrative psychologist Dan McAdams has done much to advance understanding on the storied nature of human identity. His distinctive contribution, in my opinion, is to theorize and research into the components of life stories. In his book *Power, Intimacy, and the Life Story*,[14] he advances two main points in this regard:

1) Life stories are animated by a perennial tension between the need for power, autonomy and personal agency on one hand, and for intimacy, community, and relationship on the other.[15] These are fundamental motives in life.

2) Life stories are typically constructed around:

- *Nuclear episodes*, or the landmark events in life. These are the "high points, low points, and turning points in life stories."[16]

---

[12]This was an implicit point in David Carr's challenge to Ricoeur that the latter make clear his position on the narrative quality of realities other than literary text. See David Carr, *Time, Narrative, and History*, ed. James M. Edie, Studies in Phenomenology and Existential Philosophy (Bloomington: Indiana University Press, 1986).

[13]Paul Ricoeur, "The Model of the Text: Meaningful Action Considered as a Text," *Social Research* 38, no. 3 (1971).

[14]Dan P. McAdams, *Power, Intimacy, and the Life Story: Personological Inquiries into Identity* (Homewood, Ill.: Dorsey Press, 1985).

[15]Ibid., 26.

[16]Ibid., 27.

- *Imagoes*, or "personified and idealized images of self"[17] that function as characters in our autobiographical narratives, and embody our aspirations to power and intimacy. Examples include images of oneself as a hero or victim, as a friend, as an adventurer, as a helper, or as a good citizen.
- *Ideological setting* is the "backdrop of personal beliefs and values which provides a context for … action."[18] In other words, it is what we hold as true, good and beautiful in life.
- A *generativity script*, defined as "a future plan or outline concerning what one hopes to put into life and what one hopes to get out of it to fulfill the developmental mandate of *generating* a legacy."[19] It is the component of our life story that orients us to the future and, hence, brings meaning and agency to our present.[20]

---

[17] Ibid.

[18] Ibid.

[19] Ibid (emphasis in original).

[20] McAdams further developed this thesis in *The Stories We Live By*, in which he maps the various components of identity to the stages of human development. Motivational themes of power and intimacy "may be traced back to the elementary-school years; the ideological setting is laid down in adolescence; imagoes begin to form in early adulthood; the generativity script becomes more salient as we move into mid-life." See Dan P. McAdams, *The Stories We Live By: Personal Myths and the Making of the Self* (New York: Guilford Press, 1997), 271.

His later work *The Redemptive Self* marks a shift away the conceptualization of story as relating uniquely to personal identity, to a consideration of national narratives and how they inform or constitute a nation's sense of common identity. Based on years of research, he finds common patterns in the stories that highly generative American adults tend to tell about their lives – stories that emphasize the power of human redemption and a steadfast belief that one will ultimately triumph over obstacles to find fulfillment in life. Stories of the redemptive self has an American heritage, having been embodied and articulated in foundational myths like the story of the first pilgrims, in the stories of American heroes, in literary classics, as well as in popular cultural icons like the cowboy or the space adventurer.

The attendant problem, he says, is that the redemptive self often goes hand in hand with values of individualism and exceptionalism. "The interlocking ideas of chosen people, promised land, manifest destiny, and redeemer nation form a unique constellation with an especially powerful pedigree in American cultural history – going all the way back

What are the Components of a Re-storied Narrative Identity?

How do these components of life story relate to re-storying of identity? To say that a life may be re-storied is to suggest a transformation in our sense of identity that proceeds through the psychological channels of nuclear episodes, imagoes, ideologies, and generativity scripts.

An example from my experience in faith formation ministry at Boston College (that focused on the transformative effect of immersion trips) may serve to elucidate. These trips do not always spur a re-visioning of life. But, when they are effective, they establish a new nuclear episode in students' lives – a major point of transition and one of the high points of their college experience. Moreover, these trips also occasion a rethinking of life values, coalescing around such virtues as simplicity, charity, justice and gratitude. There are newly found ideals in life that come together into new images (imagoes) of self, such as being a new person, and being blessed in life compared with so many. There may be a new sense of conviction of personal culpability in perpetuating sinful structures; all of which may give birth to an active discernment and adoption of a new generativity script – new ways of living more justly and responsibly in the world.

In conjunction with Ricoeur's thesis on the narrative mediation of identity and meaning, it is thus possible to say that encounters with the life stories of others are able to reconstitute human meaning and identity by engaging the human imagination with meaningful events, powerful and persuasive characters (imagoes), compelling ideologies, and fruitful and identifiable generativity scripts. Stories of Jesus work in this way, but so too does encountering the lived narratives of any

---

to the Puritan Myth." Dan P. McAdams, *The Redemptive Self: Stories Americans Live By* (Oxford University Press, 2006),108.

While, McAdams doesn't break down national myths into these components, I think such connections can be plausibly asserted. For instance, American national or communal myth of the redemptive self arguably revolves around nuclear episodes (such as the stories of the first Pilgrims), imagoes (the hero), ideological setting (the influence of a Christian worldview), and generativity scripts (being a world power and bastion of freedom and democracy). Moreover, U.S. foreign relations constantly discerns between the exercise of power and of intimacy (community) on the world stage.

holy person. If someone is moved by such an encounter, it is probably because that saintly figure powerfully embodied some foundational virtues like love and hope, or portrayed a life praxis that was persuasively generative, or was associated with significant events or way of life or, maybe, simply motivated a change in the way that person viewed themselves.

The problem of "There *you* are – here *I* am! How does that concern me?" is thus a problem of narrative encounter. As Ricoeur showed us, this problem masks an opportunity: new life meaning is to be gained in this encounter. But as we say "Yes!" to the narrative of the other, so can we, and often must, say "No!" As I indicated earlier, the other could come in violence and terror. What bearing, therefore, does our life in faith have on our decision of "Yes" or "No"?

Christian Conversion as Ongoing Affirmation of Discipleship to God's Self Gift

I suggest that a narrative hermeneutic is also theologically appropriate for addressing the question of otherness in our societies; it provides a way of conceptualizing how a faith that affirms (says "yes!" to) God's self-gift may be actualized in an ethic of narrative hospitality – the mutual welcoming of our storied lives.

I have thus far refrained from a definition of conversion. This can longer stand. I understand conversion as the ongoing affirmation of discipleship – our lived "yes" – to God's self-gift.[21] This "yes" is never complete, and hardly ever consistent; rather, it is *storied* by the ebbs and flows of our faith lives – by our occasions of turning away from God, by our times of indifference, and by such times when we were graced enough to respond with our whole heart, mind and soul. Our conversion story is the story of our "yes," which traces the plot of a divine-human love affair, replete with scenes of faithfulness and of our

---

[21] I should also state how I am not using the term conversion. I don't mean changing one's religious affiliation – of 'converting' to a particular creed or faith. Nor am I considering it as purely personal phenomenon; the need for communal or national conversion is probably as urgent today as it ever was.

infidelity, of reconciliation, and of God who walks in the garden of our lives calling us into deeper relationship.

I employ a Rahnerian theological ethic by claiming that we are created for this "yes," – this sacramental existential – wherein, enabled by grace, we abandon self into the Holy Mystery of God.[22] Moreover, this encounter with Holy Mystery is potentially mediated, in faith, by our encounter with the other. Paul Ricoeur, ever the theological dabbler, understood that narratives (again meaning literary text for Ricoeur) could mediate ultimate meanings and the divine presence. The parables did just that for their hearers. When Jesus wanted to communicate inexhaustible mystery – the mystery of God, or of God's reign – he told and lived (think of his table fellowship) stories. So do we! The medium of story is structurally adequate for this because it is a language form that opens up the imagination into ever expanding possibilities of meaning. Myth, Ricoeur informs, "is the bearer of other *possible* worlds."[23] Moreover, the life witness of saintly exemplars is a further example of narratives that point towards God. Thus, to the question of whether narrative can mediate a more profound understanding of God, the answer is, "yes"!

However, not all narratives are salubrious of human life; some are downright destructive and degrading. Thus, a significant qualification needs be added to the previous "yes." Even the biblical narrative, we have long recognized, warrants critical reading with a healthy hermeneutic of suspicion and retrieval.[24] In addition, the human capacity to perpetuate evil and injustice through life story and practices must also be acknowledged. Moreover, even when narratives are efficacious

---

[22]Karl Rahner, *Foundations of Christian Faith: An Introduction to the Idea of Christianity*, trans., William V. Dych (New York: The Seabury Press, 1978). See also Shannon Craigo-Snell, *Silence, Love, and Death: Saying "Yes" to God in the Theology of Karl Rahner* (Milwaukee, WI: Marquette University Press, 2008).

[23]Paul Ricoeur, "Myth as the Bearer of Possible Worlds," in *A Ricoeur Reader: Reflection and Imagination*, ed. Mario J Valdés (Toronto: University of Toronto Press, 1991), 483. Emphasis Ricoeur's.

[24]The 150th anniversary of the Declaration of Independence was a reminder of the role that the Bible played in validating the power of the slave holder, as well as its power to incite liberation.

in leading human beings closer to God, they are ultimately and inevitably insufficient to that task. No narrative, no matter how provocative, is sufficient for the task of mediating the awesome majesty and mystery of God. To think otherwise is idolatry.

Saying "yes" to God in the context of our age means greater openness and hospitality to the other, as well as greater risk and uncertainty. We are called to leave the certainties of our own finite existence and risk that the presence of the other may occasion a transformative encounter with grace. This is the existential wager demanded by faith in a God who comes shrouded in mystery and otherness.

Narrative and Conversion: Re-storying our Faith Lives in Response to God

To say that conversion is a re-storying of our lives in faith is to say that it is a refiguring of our sense of who we are before God. It is growing in knowledge of our finitude, our sinfulness, but also our giftedness and created dignity. Moreover, we may come to this knowledge as we discern God's presence in the ordinary experiences of life, and as we open to the life events, imagoes, values and generative themes of the human other.

At the start of this essay, I laid out some thick questions imposed by that story on our thinking on conversion, namely: How do the claims embodied in difference or otherness contextualize and make concrete the demands of discipleship as ongoing conversion in faith? My best answer, from a narrative perspective, is that the claim made by the other regards our "yes." *To say yes is to welcome the story of the other. It is to practice narrative hospitality.* What does this mean? In a general sense, it means that we must attend, with a critical mind and with responsibility, to how others are implicated and affected by the narratives that we live, and to how we are implicated in others' stories by choice or by chance. We ought to attend to how our lives impact others for good or for ill, and to how the stories that our neighbors live impose upon us. This means rejecting the injurious narratives that we inherit or in which we are implicated, personally and through the discourse and actions of community, institution and nation.

Let me make two specific suggestions regarding the practice of narrative hospitality that may be of relevance to our discipleship and educating in faith. First, as persons and as a nation we need to do better at practicing *temporal hospitality*. This means that, as persons and as a nation, we recognize our place in historical community. We ordinarily do this through our establishment of museums and erection of monuments and statues. However, temporal hospitality is more encompassing and more challenging. It means recognizing *the burden of the past*: that the possibilities of life that we enjoy today rest on the legacy of the silent majority who came before us. Temporal hospitality especially means keeping the storied memory of the oppressed of history alive, as a barometer for our own moral decision-making. It means living the gospel story in the present with agency, responsibility and fidelity and, as such, rendering our own stories as compelling witnesses to the truth of God's love and forgiveness. Finally, to practice temporal hospitality is to be a good steward of the future. It demands striving for a just, sustainable world where our progeny too may flourish and have the opportunity to be their best God-given selves.

Second, as a nation, we also need to do better in the practice of *spatial hospitality*. We need to create what Letty Russell called safe spaces where hospitality can be practiced.[25] What do I mean by that? We need spaces where we can encounter the stories of others, our neighbors, in all their richness, complexities, tragedies and victories. There are too many non-spaces that proliferate our landscape. Malls and supermarkets define us solely as consumers, separating us only by our spending ability and preferences. On the highways and airports of life, we are travelers, differentiated by our ability to pay for five inches of additional leg-room, or for a five-minute earlier boarding time. The proliferation of such spaces may make our societies more efficient, but only at the cost of defining us, beyond our ability-to-pay, as an amorphous crowd. We are continually dehumanized inasmuch as the din of market efficiency muffles our uniqueness and particularity.

---

[25]Letty M. Russell, *Just Hospitality: God's Welcome in a World of Difference*, ed. J. Shannon Clarkson and Kate M. Ott (Loiusville, KY: Westminster John Knox Press, 2009), 85.

To practice spatial hospitality is to humanize by being attentive to what most embodies human selfhood – our story! How wonderful would it be to reimagine common spaces where we can practice narrative empathy[26] – telling and living our stories, and listening and welcoming the storied lives of others? In pursuit of this, we ought to take a searching look at how well traditional settings like our church communities offer hospitality and neighbor-love. Yet, we ought also to extend, imaginatively, this practice to non-traditional settings. Take, for example, our supermarkets. In day-to-day life we are, more often than not, unaware of the source of our food, and of the stories of the agricultural workers who wrestle with multinational corporations for a living wage. To practice spatial hospitality is to get to know the transcontinental stories behind the products that we consume, and to promote global justice through practices like fair trade. Conversion that is responsive to the global-present rests in the active affirmation that we all share a common human story, and that this should concern us all.

The story we build together may be unknown, unfinished, swaddled in uncertainty and mystery. Yet, ultimately, it is God's story in which we share, and to which we are responsible. It is the unfolding story of God's reign in history and society. The wager of cultivating narrative hospitality to the other (spatial and temporal) is that grace will be ever present. The promise of such conversion is a more profound knowledge of the mystery of God and of human being. This isn't the only invitation and challenge of contemporary discipleship. But surely it is a worthy one.

---

[26]Suzanne Keen, "A Theory of Narrative Empathy," *Narrative* 14, no. 3 (2006).

Bibliography

Bruner, Jerome S. *Actual Minds, Possible Worlds*. Cambridge, MA.: Harvard University Press, 1986.

_____."The Narrative Construction of "Reality"." In *Psychoanalysis and Development: Representations and Development*, edited by Massimo Ammaniti and Daniel N. Stern, 15-38. New York: New York University Press, 1994.

Carr, David. *Time, Narrative, and History* Studies in Phenomenology and Existential Philosophy, Edited by James M. Edie. Bloomington: Indiana University Press, 1986.

Craigo-Snell, Shannon. *Silence, Love, and Death: Saying "Yes" to God in the Theology of Karl Rahner*. Milwaukee, WI: Marquette University Press, 2008.

Crites, Stephen. "Storytime: Recollecting the Past and Projecting the Future." In *Narrative Psychology: The Storied Nature of Human Conduct*, edited by Theodore R. Sarbin, 152-73. New York: Praeger, 1986.

_____."The Narrative Quality of Experience." In *Why Narrative?: Readings in Narrative Theology*, edited by Stanley Hauerwas and L. Gregory Jones, 65-88. Grand Rapids, Mich.: W.B. Eerdmans, 1989.

Ganz, Marshall. "Why Stories Matter: The Art and Craft of Social Change." *Sojourners Magazine* 38, no. 3 (2009): 16-21.

Groome, Thomas H. *Christian Religious Education: Sharing Our Story and Vision*. 1st ed. San Francisco: Harper & Row, 1980.

Huntington, Samuel P. *The Clash of Civilizations and the Remaking of World Order*. New York: Simon & Schuster, 2003.

_____.*Who Are We?: The Challenges to America's National Identity*. New York: Simon & Schuster Paperbacks, 2004.

Jüngel, Eberhard. "The Effectiveness of Christ Withdrawn: On the Process of Historical Understanding as an Introduction to Christology." In *Theological Essays I*, edited by J. B. Webster, 214-231. Edinburgh, Scotland: T & T Clark, 1989.

Keen, Suzanne. "A Theory of Narrative Empathy." *Narrative* 14, no. 3 (2006): 207-236.

McAdams, Dan P. *Power, Intimacy, and the Life Story: Personological Inquiries into Identity.* Homewood, Ill.: Dorsey Press, 1985.

_____. *The Stories We Live By: Personal Myths and the Making of the Self.* New York: Guilford Press, 1997.

_____. *The Redemptive Self: Stories Americans Live By.* Oxford: Oxford University Press, 2006.

Pellauer, David. "Limning the Liminal: Carr and Ricoeur on Time and Narrative." *Philosophy Today* 35, no. 1 (1991: Spring): 51-62.

Polkinghorne, Donald. *Narrative Knowing and the Human Sciences.* Suny Series in Philosophy of the Social Sciences, Edited by Lenore Langsdorf. Albany: State University of New York Press, 1988.

Rahner, Karl. *Foundations of Christian Faith: An Introduction to the Idea of Christianity.* Translated by William V. Dych. New York: The Seabury Press, 1978.

Ricoeur, Paul. "The Model of the Text: Meaningful Action Considered as a Text." *Social Research* 38, no. 3 (1971): 529-562.

_____. *Time and Narrative.* Translated by Kathleen Blamey and David Pellauer. 3 vols. Chicago: The University of Chicago Press, 1984-1988.

_____. "Life in Quest of Narrative." In *On Paul Ricoeur: Narrative and Interpretation*, edited by David Wood, 20-33. London: Routledge, 1991.

_____. "Myth as the Bearer of Possible Worlds." In *A Ricoeur Reader: Reflection and Imagination*, edited by Mario J Valdés, 482-490. Toronto: University of Toronto Press, 1991.

Russell, Letty M. *Just Hospitality: God's Welcome in a World of Difference*, Edited by J. Shannon Clarkson and Kate M. Ott. Loiusville, KY: Westminster John Knox Press, 2009.

Sarbin, Theodore R., ed. *Narrative Psychology: The Storied Nature of Human Conduct.* New York: Praeger, 1986.

Schrag, Calvin O. *Communicative Praxis and the Space of Subjectivity.* Bloomington: Indiana University Press, 1986.

Sen, Amartya. *Identity and Violence: The Illusion of Destiny.* New York: Norton, 2007.

Volf, Miroslav. *Exclusion and Embrace: A Theological Exploration of Identity, Otherness, and Reconciliation.* Nashville: Abingdon Press, 1996.

Emerging from the Vineyard. Essays by Lay Ecclesial Ministers. Edited by Maureen R. O'Brien and Susan Yanos. Fortuity Press, 2014. 225 pages. (paper)

In 2005, the United States Conference of Catholic Bishops voted on guidelines for formation of lay ecclesial ministers in the Church. These guidelines formed the document "Coworkers in the Vineyard of the Lord". Since this time, many dioceses, parishes, schools of ministry and theology have used this document as a guide for the formation of lay ministers in the Catholic Church. Since the promulgation of the document, a wealth of books has been published addressing lay ecclesial ministry and theology. Such theologians as Zeni Fox (*Lay Ecclesial Ministry: Pathways Towards the Future,* Sheed and Ward, 2010), Edward Hannenberg (*Theology of Ministry,* Liturgical Press, 2014)and Aurelie Hagstrom (*Emerging Laity: The Vocation, Mission and Spirituality,* Paulist Press, 2010) have contributed to this landscape bringing much needed attention to the role of lay ecclesial ministers in the Church today.

While the above mentioned books have been excellent resources, what has been lacking has been a book about lay ecclesial ministers from those LEMs who are themselves working in the vineyard. This changes with the publication of the new book, Emerging *from the Vineyard. Essays by Lay Ecclesial Ministers*, (Fortuity Press, 2014) edited by Duquesne University professor Maureen O'Brien and Professor Susan Yanos of Earlham School of Religion. The publication of this book emerged from a grant from Duquesne University in 2010 awarded to the editors for further research on lay ecclesial ministry. The monies used for the grant funded a series of weekend gatherings of 10 lay ministers focused on lay ecclesial ministry. These gatherings in the context of prayer, discussion resulted in the collaborative writing and review of the essays which are included in this book. This collection of essays addresses some of the challenges of being in the vineyard as well as the question of whether there 'has there been any fruit from the vineyard' that can nourish a hungry community?

The book opens with an introduction by O'Brien which addresses the context and the various themes which are the topics of the essays found in this book. As she states, the ten essays "reflect a blending of ten individual commitments, within the common commitment of the group writers, to explore key theological dimensions of their ministry, for the sake of all lay ecclesial ministers and those who foster their service" (17).

Section One focuses attention on the ministerial identity of the laity and looks at the foundational aspect of the call to lay ministry. Both authors in this section address the lay minister as one whose identity stems from the biblical narratives found in the New Testament. While the ordained minister has used the model of Jesus for an understanding of ministry, Jerid Miller in his article "With Jesus and His Companions: At the Genesis of Lay Ministry" addresses the question of whether Jesus has status as a lay person. As he states "many of the questions about contemporary manifestations of lay ministry ignore a fundamental reality –that lay ministry and lay ministers go back to the very source of our identity as Christians, to Jesus himself (36). This provocative statement is just one of many found in the pages of this book.

Section Two: Ministry of Word and Works focuses on the ministerial actions of the lay ecclesial minister. Essays by Kimberly Lymore, Linda Lee Ritzer and Rodney Blumi address the role of minister as an agent for social change and the peculiar role the lay minister holds as one who is called to preach and proclaim the Good News.

In Section Three: Transformation through Ministry, Dan Frachey, Virginia Stillwell and Vivian Clausing address the spiritual dimensions of lay ecclesial ministry specifically through its baptismal identity, as well as focusing on its Eucharistic aspects and its connection to the Paschal Mystery.

Finally in Section Four: Communal Call and Authorization for Ministry the essays by Julie M. Billmeier and Susan Yanos address young adults' response to a call to ministry in the church as well as the challenge both financially and emotionally in responding to become a lay ecclesial minister today in the Catholic Church.

Of particular note are the questions for reflection and discussion included at the end of each chapter. These questions specifically invite the readers to reflect upon their own particular context while engaged in the reading of the material. As a reviewer, one area of concern is the limited voices attached to the essays in this book. Except for two of the articles written by African American scholar Kimberly Lymore and Young Adult scholar Julie M. Billmeier, most of the essays still address a "homogenous" view of church from a white middle class perspective. It would have been a stronger book if the editors had expanded the essays to include perspectives from the African, Latino, Caribbean, Asian or gay and lesbian community in this book.

As a practical theologian of ministry and spirituality who teaches a course on the spirituality and ministry of the lay vocation at a graduate school of ministry, I believe this book will be an invaluable resource for students preparing for ministry in the church. I furthermore highly recommend it for all those who teach, minister with and/or are lay ministers in the church.

Dr. C. Vanessa White
Catholic Theological Union
Chicago, Illinois

Introducing African American Religion. Anthony B. Pinn. New York: Routledge, 2013. 276. $39.95. Paper. ISBN: 978-415-69401.

Introducing African American Religion, by prolific religious studies scholar, Anthony B. Pinn is a welcome find. This textbook is part of Routledge's World Religions Series, and it comes complete with illustrations, summary points embedded within the text, summary questions and a bibliography at the end of each chapter, discussion questions, a glossary, and chronology. At the end of the text Pinn also provides websites, movies, music, and YouTube video links all pointing to an engaging multiplatform approach to African American Religion in all its diversity.

IAAR is divided into three parts. I. "The nature, origins, and historical overview of African American religion;" II. "Major themes in African American religions;" and III. "Issues and concerns in contemporary African American religion." (v-vi) The first two parts are adequately broad and engage Islam, African traditional religions, Judaism, and secular humanism, in addition to Christianity. An important and necessary third part provides sustained attention to sex and sexuality, hip hop and religion, and the new "nones," those who do not claim a particular religious tradition or community.

This book works because of Pinn's expansive definition of African American religion as "the effort to make life meaningful and to do so in response to the questions we ask about our existence and the world in which we live" (13). While some might be more inclined to use Pinn's definition to speak about spirituality, he is curiously enough content to include humanism under the category of African American religion. A leitmotif that runs through this book is the importance of underrepresented groups, such as humanists. Roman Catholics and other groups benefit from Pinn's attention.

IAAR is a user friendly book that will appeal to visual learners. This characteristic is particularly necessary since African American religion is best explained within its historical context. Pinn writes a narrative that is clear and straight forward. Additionally, his list of books for further reading at the end of each chapter includes important classic texts that could further enhance the main themes addressed in the chapters.

While Pinn is at pains to identify evidence of the presence of humanism in African American history, this is not always clear prior to the twentieth century. While some work songs and the blues sung during slavery may emphasize human agency or question the action of God, these themes are not mutually exclusive of belief in God or other divinities.

In the chapter on the twentieth century, Pinn very effectively mentions "humanist sensibilities" evident in the literature of Harlem Renaissance authors such as Richard Wright, and later authors such as Lorraine Hansberry, and Alice Walker (94). He also points to the presence of humanists within the Civil Rights Movement. Later in the text, current and recent religious realities are treated, such as, Jeremiah Wright, the so-called "prosperity gospel," and the different forms of liberation theology that are a part of African American religion.

In the concluding chapter on the new nones, Pinn addresses the importance of the inclusion of atheists in a book on African American religion. While acknowledging the challenge of some to place non-theists under the moniker of religion, Pinn identifies four reasons why the inclusion of nones is important to give a thick description of the African American religious landscape. 1) Religion, whether on is suspicious about it or opts out of being connected with it is important to the self-identity of nones. 2) The growth in African American nones signals changes in the religious experience of African Americans. 3) By considering the existence of nones, all are able to give consideration to other paths to lifelong meaning making. 4) Despite strong differences between theists and non-theists, many dimensions of their lives are intertwined as both groups are about the work of finding and sustaining meaning in life (236).

I would recommend *Introducing African American Religion* as a text that is inclusive of effective pedagogical approaches. Pinn accomplishes quite a bit in the 276 pages of the text and prompts his readers to be attentive to the changing landscape of African American religions.

Dr. LaReine-Marie Mosely
Notre Dame of Maryland University
Baltimore, Maryland

Presumed Incompetent: The Intersections of Race and Class for Women in Academia. Yolanda Flores, Angela Harris, Gabriela Gutierrez y Muhs and Carmen Gonzales, editors. Boulder, CO: Utah State University Press, 2012. 512. Paperback 0874219221. $38.95

Presumed Incompetent: The Intersections of Race and Class for Women in Academia examines the effects of race and gender on female faculty members in institutions of higher education. It is a compilation of personal stories, a majority of which are from women of color sharing their pain, struggles, disappointments, and challenges within the environment of academia which is clouded with racism and classism. This would include fellow faculty/staff members and students with whom they work and commune on a daily basis. These women of color have achieved the highest degree, yet experience racism and inequalities that are alive and well in the 21st century.

The book is divided into five major sections that address critical issues that affect academics of color: General Campus Climate, Faculty/Student Relationships, Networks of Allies, Social Class in Academia, and Tenure and Promotion. The fact that many of those invited declined to participate because of fears of retaliation or breaking academia's code of silence brings home the valuable contribution this work makes to the much needed discussion on the pressures and perils of being both female and persons of color in academia today. The editors note that "Our goal as editors was to empower women of color and allies by providing tools and strategies to overcome the challenges described in this volume." [3]

There are three major areas which I would like to address that became themes for me throughout the book: the climate for African-American women within the educational field; faculty/student relationships; and tenure and promotions.

For women of color, a basic perception of incompetence is presumed on college and university campuses because of the color of their skin. It is noted that the conscious and subconscious understandings of racism are at work in the minds of many white people who are seen as the privileged class within our society. Because of this bias, the white, male-dominated hierarchy within academia has often created a hostile and intimidating environment for people of color. Behaviors can be condescending in language, as well as attitude. African-American male educators [have] gained some access to this "private club" since the Civil Rights Movement and Affirmative Action, but this gave way to an attitude of resentment from the original members which currently makes life even more difficult for the African-American female working in such institutions.

Women of color who do not have strong and enduring backbones will not be able to survive the test of time within these corridors of academia. Their encounters will create stressors that affect the mind, body and soul. The authors note that some of the women who have experienced negative behavior gave way to despair, and for some that despair resulted even in taking their own lives. A solid support system for Black and other women of color in this kind of oppressive atmosphere is of critical importance. The work's last chapter provides examples and recommendations.

Contributors attest to the fact that Caucasian students, too often, have viewed these women as incompetent based on their skin color and their own lack of experience with people of color. This perception gives many students the opportunity to infuse their own personal bias and stereotypes into the classroom, challenging their professors because they feel and think they do not have the knowledge to teach on the university level. These stereotypes are unintentionally reinforced at times because of possible outward differences: in terms of wardrobe, braided hairstyles, or maybe even the professors' choice of expression. If this kind of student/faculty experience exists, it can possibly give the students more power over a woman of color through student evaluations, thus reducing even further her feelings of self-worth and her colleagues' and others negative perspective of them. If there is no support from fellow faculty members, this tool of evaluation from the students is another opportunity for the administrators to dismiss a female professor of color.

This same notion of tokenism and stereotypes for the women of color in academia makes its way through the thick layers of tenure and promotion. Being female and African-American can seem like two strikes against them when dealing with the white, male-dominated institutions in which they work.

In addition to putting more stake in student evaluations than normal for the purpose of not granting tenure or promotions, for many administrators and faculty members in predominant universities, the text asserts that it is common practice to marginalize them and find ways to keep them isolated or give these women of color overbearing and inflexible hours to maintain outside the classroom – such as additional workloads to teach in the summer and having long office hours or other burdensome requirements that white academics don't have to face. These factors can lead to even more exclusion and isolation.

In spite of the many obstacles placed in the paths of women of color in academia, the work reveals that solutions are available. Mentoring is essential for survival in the institutional system as is an understanding of self that includes the "double consciousness" professed by Du Bois--being capable of working out of both worlds, white and black, while embracing both the African-American and female aspects of the experience; knowing what is going on around you; sharpening political skills; giving back to the community through service; forging strong connections with biological and extended family around and outside of them; encouraging all faculty members to participate in and encourage the teaching of controversial and emotionally charged topics within their own courses; being involved in programs that take care of their mental and physical health; and setting up a social network in order to create a structure of trust, communication, and support so that others do not have to live in isolation or desolation are viable examples. It is noted that when anyone lives under these kinds of conditions of overt racism, their psychological well-being affects their job performance, thus making it extremely difficult to achieve the ultimate of one's potential.

Most of the women who participated in this book continue to thrive with great dignity under these extremely daunting circumstances. It is only when you go through the pressures of life that one is able to resurrect with a stronger ability to articulate that struggle and express an insight into a life that gives it authenticity. The personal stories in this book reveal that all people of color have a personal story of struggle and redemption to share with the world. In sharing their story, the pain and burden of oppression is made a bit lighter.

I believe that most African-Americans, male or female, as well as other persons of color in the United States can relate to *Presumed Incompetent* because the experiences of racism and inequality set forth in its pages are part of the fabric woven for all people of color in this country. Beginning to solve the problems that women of color encounter as educators in academic institutions is to first become aware of what is happening. *Presumed Incompetent* does just that. It opens the door for dialogue so that the burden can be lightened, thus leading hopefully to obstacles being removed. This, in turn, allows African-American and other women of color in universities all over America to be respected, promoted, and most importantly empowered to do their fundamental job: Educate.

This work is a valuable and critical addition to the growing literature on the roles that prejudice and discrimination continue to play in academia in the United States. It is vital reading for anyone in academia or planning to enter, regardless of race, ethnicity, or gender.

Fr. Roy Lee
St. Leo's University
Atlanta, Georgia

BCTS ANNUAL MEETINGS

2014 Catholic Theological Union, Chicago, Illinois

2013 Bellarmine University, Louisville, Kentucky

2012 St. Thomas University, Miami Gardens, Florida

2011 Marquette University, Milwaukee, Wisconsin

2010 Stetson University, DeLand, Florida

2009 Atlanta University, Atlanta, Georgia

2008 Catholic Theological Union and Loyola University, Chicago, Illinois

2007 St. Meinrad Archabbey, St. Meinrad, Indiana

2006 Boston College, Boston, Massachusetts

2005 St. Mary's Seminary at the University of St. Thomas and St. Francis of Assisi Parish, Houston, Texas

2004 Xavier University, New Orleans, Louisiana

2003 Atlanta University, Atlanta, Georgia

2002 Gonzaga University, Spokane, Washington

2001 University of Dayton, Dayton, Ohio

2000 Marquette University, Milwaukee, Wisconsin

1999 University of Notre Dame, Notre Dame, Indiana

1998 Marquette University, Milwaukee, Wisconsin

1997 No meeting

1996   The University of San Diego, San Diego, California

1995   St. John University, New York, New York.
        Met in conjunction with ACHTUS (Academy of
        Hispanic Theologians in the United States)

1994   Mt. Vernon, Hotel, Baltimore, Maryland

1993   The Mexican American Cultural Center
        San Antonio, Texas

1992   Duquesne University, Pittsburgh, Pennsylvania

1991   The Atlanta University Complex, Atlanta, Georgia

1979   Second Meeting of the BCTS
        Motherhouse of the Oblate Sisters of Providence
        Baltimore, Maryland

1978   First Meeting of the BCTS
        Motherhouse of the Oblate Sisters of Providence
        Baltimore, Maryland

www.ingramcontent.com/pod-product-compliance
Lightning Source LLC
Chambersburg PA
CBHW071624170426
43195CB00038B/2118